Inner Child

Recovery Workbook

Heal Childhood Trauma, Abandonment, Neglect, and Abuse. Includes Prompts, Exercises and Activities to Overcome Trust Issues, Low Self-Esteem and Cultivate Self-Love

Linda Hill

Table of Content

Introduction

As children, all of us experienced trauma in some form. The trauma I speak of can be as obvious as physical and sexual abuse or as subtle as medical issues, accidents, poverty, or bullying. These traumas remain with us into adulthood unless they are addressed.

The challenge is that many of these memories are subconscious, so we are unaware of them. Though we may not be aware of these memories, their energy affects us daily. Many of our stronger emotional responses result from these memories being triggered.

What is referred to as your "inner child" holds these memories. Healing your inner child entails bringing resolution to these memories. To do so requires that the light of your awareness be allowed to illuminate them and integrate them with your conscious self. Once these memories are integrated, you will no longer be triggered by them.

Doing inner child work offers incredible potential for personal growth. When your inner child remains in the subconscious, its reactivity will be reflected in your decisions and actions. Your adult mind may rationalize your decisions and actions, but you are justifying something beyond your awareness.

Inner child work involves confronting and understanding these memories. In doing so, your adult mind takes charge of them. When this occurs, your inner child will function to support your happiness.

This kind of healing will occur not only from within but also externally. Your inner child work will show up in the improved quality of your relationships and other areas of your life. The reason for this is simple. Your inner child has tinted your view of yourself and the world around you. That view is tinted with fear.

When you do inner child work, this tinted lens is replaced by clarity and understanding. Your increased confidence and self-knowledge will show up in how you engage with the world around you.

This workbook will provide you with simple but powerful exercises that will allow you to access your inner child and give them the recognition and care they have been deprived of. In doing so, you will be able to take back your personal power while at the same time providing parenting to your inner child, which they never had.

However, to do inner child work effectively, you need to be honest with yourself, be willing to face strong emotions, and be determined to hang in there until the end. While it may be difficult in the short term, the benefits you will get in the long term will be huge. Besides, if you do not address your inner child, you will prolong your suffering into the future. You have everything to gain and nothing to lose. The journey starts now for you to reclaim the authenticity of who you are.

CHAPTER 1

Understanding Your Inner Child

You will begin this chapter by gaining a deeper understanding of your inner child. As you will see, your inner child is simply an aspect of yourself that you have repressed.

Exploring the Inner Child

Janet is a young child whose parents are often critical of her and inconsistent in showing her affection. In her attempts to appease her parents, Janet starts to repress those aspects of herself that her parents are critical of and starts to adopt those they approve of. As she continues these efforts, the adopted features become more and more ingrained in her sense of identity while the repressed ones are pushed deeper into her subconscious.

Though Janet's sense of identity has been molded by her adopted aspects, the suppressed ones retain their energies. These energies will continue to affect her emotionally and her decision-making. For example, let's say that one of Janet's natural traits is to be easygoing. Her parents view this critically because they believe that being easygoing will make their daughter an easy target for others to take advantage of. They also believe you can never be successful with an easygoing personality.

Janet picks up on the displeasure of her parents and starts to adopt an attitude where she pushes herself and becomes more competitive. As Janet gets older, she will think and behave in ways that reflect these qualities. They will become a part of her personal identity. When she meets someone easygoing, she will view them in a negative way. She will see them in the same way that her parents saw her.

The reason Janet views such individuals this way is that they remind her of her suppressed qualities. Janet is projecting the energies of these suppressed qualities onto others. Her negative view of these individuals has nothing to do with the individuals themselves. Rather, she is reacting to her suppressed self. The easygoing individuals are eliciting the energies of Janet's suppressed memories. As these energies bring about an uncomfortable feeling, she attributes these feelings to the individuals.

This scenario of Janet represents how our unresolved suppressed memories impact our life experiences. Additionally, these suppressed memories are authentic aspects of ourselves. We cannot be authentic as people until we learn to accept all aspects of ourselves.

Exercise 1: Know Your Intentions

Directions: The following are writing prompts to help you get to know your inner child. Choose one or more of the following writing prompts and write about them.

- When doing inner child work, I think I will have the most difficulty with the following:

- When becoming honest with myself, I think the most difficult thing for me to face will be:

- What I most want to change about myself when doing inner child work is:

- My intentions for learning to heal my inner child are:

_____

_____

Recognizing Childhood Patterns

To recognize your childhood patterns, it is important that you listen to your inner child. You can do that by paying attention to what you are experiencing when situations bring out strong emotions in you.

Emotions you may experience include:

- Anger

- Rejection or abandonment

- Insecurity

- Shame

- Guilt

- Vulnerability

- Anxiety

Try to trace the emotions you are experiencing back to their original source—a specific childhood experience. You can then see how that emotional response gets triggered in your adult life.

I remember once how I asked my wife if she would help me out with a problem I was having. Because she was going through a difficult time, she turned down my request. I remember feeling rejected and alone. I started writing about this experience and reflecting on my childhood. I remember feeling the same way when I approached my parents with a request, and they turned me down.

The feelings I experienced when my wife turned down my request were grounded in the wounds of my inner child.

Have you experienced something like this in your life? Do you notice yourself experiencing patterns of behavior or thinking that do not support you in becoming happy? Perhaps you can identify with some of the following patterns of thinking or behaviors:

- You experience fear when there is no rational reason for it.

- You have perfectionist tendencies.

- You tend to feel anxious in your relationships.

- You tend to avoid becoming emotionally intimate with others.

- You tend to be demanding in your relationships and try to control your partner.

These are just a few examples of thinking and behavioral patterns you may use when you are feeling unsafe. They are responses triggered by childhood memories, some of which may be subconscious. While these patterns may have served you as a child by making you feel safe, they serve no purpose for you as an adult. They prevent you from experiencing fulfillment and happiness.

Exercise 2: What Do You Want to Change?

Directions: Choose one or more of the following writing prompts to identify the patterns of thinking or behavior that you would like to change:

- I want to give up my resistance toward:

- I want to no longer feel triggered by:

- The part of me that I want to learn to accept and be at peace with is:

Exercise 3: Journaling to Channel Your Inner Child

Writing can be a powerful way to deal with confusing or challenging experiences. It can help you process and clarify your experiences. In this way, writing can also help you gain access to your inner child.

Keeping a journal can help you recognize patterns which you may want to change. Many of these patterns may have developed in childhood. To identify the patterns you have kept, try journaling from the viewpoint of your inner child. The following exercise will guide you through this process:

1. Identify a pattern of behavior or thinking that you want to change.

2. To the best of your ability, determine when you may have adopted this pattern.

3. Step out of your adult frame of mind and reconnect with yourself as a child. You can do this by looking at a childhood photo or by visualizing yourself as a child.

4. When you have accessed your childhood mindset, write down any memories you have of the events that occurred at that age. Also, write down any emotions you remember experiencing that were associated with those events.

5. When writing, do not think about it too much. Instead, write down whatever comes to mind. Let your writing flow as thoughts appear. By doing this, you will gain insight into your inner child's pain.

Chapter Writing Prompts

Inner child writing prompts can be a powerful way to access your subconscious mind and connect with your inner child. When a writing prompt asks you to write from the child's viewpoint, try your best to step out of your adult mindset and try to perceive the situation through the child's eyes.

When you have accessed your childhood mindset, write down any memories you have of the events that occurred at that age. Also, write down any emotions you remember experiencing that were associated with those events.

When writing, do not think about it too much. Instead, write down whatever comes to mind. Let your writing flow as your thoughts appear. By doing this, you will gain insight into your inner child's pain.

Choose from the writing prompts below and respond to them in your journal.

1. In your mind, visualize yourself as a child. As you visualize this, what do you notice? How does the child feel? What emotions come up when you imagine this?

2. If you could speak to your inner child at this moment, what would you tell them? What can you do to offer them support, love, or reassurance?

3. What could you do to reconnect with your body and support your inner child's physical well-being?

4. As a child, were there boundaries that you had difficulty with? How have those boundaries affected you as an adult?

CHAPTER 2

Nurturing Your Inner Child

In Chapter 1, you began an inquiry about your inner child by identifying the patterns of thoughts and behaviors that do not support your happiness. Your inner child adopted these patterns to feel safe. However, these patterns no longer support your happiness. The challenge is that we resist facing our inner child because the inner child is a source of painful memories. It is easier to rationalize or deny this pain's existence than face it.

Your inner child has been abandoned. You have disowned it by repressing its existence. The only way to feel like you are being your authentic self is to reconnect with your inner child and build trust. The following sections will guide you on how to start the process.

Creating a Safe Space

Before you can heal your inner child, you first need to gain its trust. From a psychological perspective, you need to be more compassionate with yourself. You can be more compassionate toward yourself by stopping judging yourself and being kind to yourself. By doing so, you will create less resistance toward yourself. By lowering your resistance to yourself, you will be better able to understand the needs of your inner child.

The following exercises are intended to generate greater self-compassion and bring about relaxation or self-soothing. Learning how to do these things will allow you to regulate your emotions whenever you find yourself triggered by your subconscious memories.

Exercise 1: Validating Your Inner Child

Directions:

1. In the spaces provided below, list the names of those you love and care about or those who make you feel safe.

_____

_____

_____

_____

_____

_____

_____

_____

_____

_____

_____

_____

_____

_____

_____

_____

_____

_____

_____

_____

2. Next, get relaxed. You can do that by taking a couple of deep breaths. When you feel relaxed, imagine yourself as a child and surrounded by the people you listed in Step 1.

As you imagine the people on your list, hear them tell you the following:

- "You make me so happy."

- "You're so special to me."

- "I want to take care of all your needs."

- "I will always be here for you."

- "I will keep you safe."

- "I am so proud of you."

- "You are so beautiful."

As you hear these words, pay attention to the feelings you are experiencing. Embrace those feelings and know that you are loved and accepted.

Exercise 2: Being Mindful of Breath

Being mindful of the breath is one of the oldest methods for calming the mind. It also demonstrates compassion for yourself and is a way to soothe yourself.

Directions: To do this exercise, do the following:

1. Get into a comfortable position.

2. Inhale deeply and exhale slowly. Repeat this step three times.

3. Breathe normally.

4. Close your eyes and place your attention on your breath. Notice the sensations you experience in your body as you breathe in and out.

5. Whenever you find yourself distracted by your thoughts, return your attention to your breath.

6. Repeat this exercise daily until you feel comfortable and reach a calm state. After that, you can use it whenever you feel you need it.

Exercise 3: Write a Letter to Honor Yourself

Directions: In the space below, do the following:

1. Make a list of eight qualities that you most like about yourself. Examples of qualities may include:

   • Aspects of your physical appearance.

   • Aspects of your personality.

   • Things that you have done in the past that you are proud of.

   • Any knowledge, skills, or talents that you may have.

2. Next, list how these qualities have benefited you in the past.

3. Finally, think about what you could do to honor those qualities.

_____

_____

_____

_____

_____

_____

Exercise 4: Create a Self-Care Plan

Directions: To create the self-care plan, do the following:

1. Make a list of the activities that give you a sense of well-being.

When choosing your activities, include two types of activities: impromptu and planned.

Impromptu activities are ones that you can do anywhere at any time. Examples include:

- Breathing exercises

- Running

- Meditation

- Walking

Planned activities may require special equipment or a specific time or place. Examples include:

- Hiking

- Swimming

- Going to dinner or the movies

- Spending time with friends

- Getting a massage

2. When you have completed your list, make two copies. Keep one copy at home. Post this copy in a place where you will see it every day. This will serve as a reminder for you. Keep the second copy on your person so you will have it whenever you are out.

3. Commit each day to doing at least one of your activities.

Reconnecting with Playfulness and Joy

In the previous section, you did exercises to create a safe place for yourself. This safe place is where you can calm yourself and validate your feelings. It is also a space for affirming your self-worth. By doing this, you have established a foundation to permit yourself to play and experience joy.

Allowing yourself to play and experience joy is a way of nurturing your inner child and your subconscious memories that see validation.

Instead of resisting these memories and the feelings they evoke, you focus on play and enjoyment. This is important for connecting with your inner child's subconscious memories.

The following exercises will allow your adult self to remember what it is like to play again. Remember, part of inner child healing is experiencing those things that your inner child may have missed out on. You will begin moving beyond your wounded child by learning how to play again.

Exercise 5: Bringing Back the Good Times!

Directions: Use the space below to write down all the activities you used to have fun doing but gave up. When you complete your list, reincorporate them into your daily life.

_____

_____

_____

_____

Chapter Writing Prompts

Inner child writing prompts can be a powerful way to access your subconscious mind and connect with your inner child. When a writing prompt asks you to write from the child's viewpoint, try your best to step out of your adult mindset and try to perceive the situation through the child's eyes.

When you have accessed your childhood mindset, write down any memories you have of the events that occurred at that age. Also, write down any emotions you remember experiencing that were associated with those events.

When writing, do not think about it too much. Instead, write down whatever comes to mind. Let your writing flow as thoughts appear. By doing this, you will gain insight into your inner child's pain.

Choose from the writing prompts below and respond to them in your journal.

1. Rewrite your childhood narrative the way you would like it to be. What does your rewritten childhood narrative look like? How would your life change if you lived by your new narrative?

2. What made you feel powerless as a child? What could you do to reclaim your power and support your inner child?

3. If you could create a safe and nurturing environment for your inner child, what would that environment look like? How could you make that environment real for you?

4. What childhood memories do you have that need healing? How could you revisit those memories and provide comfort to your inner child?

5. What negative or distorted beliefs did your inner child take on? What could you do to challenge and change those beliefs?

CHAPTER 3

Healing Emotional Wounds

In Chapter 1 of this workbook, you learned that each of us has childhood memories that are retained into adulthood. Sometimes those memories are painful, resulting in their being suppressed and unconscious. Though unconscious, their memories continue to affect our lives. These unconscious memories are within our inner child.

In Chapter 2, you learned about nurturing your inner child by providing them with a safe space and the opportunity to play and have fun. You allowed your adult self to engage in these feelings and behaviors. In this chapter, you will learn about healing your inner child.

How Do I Heal My Inner Child?

Everyone has a wounded inner child, as no parent is perfect, no matter how much they loved and supported you. For example, a child may have had parents who worked most of the time to support them.

While the parents worked hard to give their child the best life possible, their absence may have created an emotional wound in the child that became subconscious. The ability of adults to parent is only as great as their level of awareness. In turn, parents carry the wounded inner child they received from their parents. As adults, our wounded inner child may take on the form of our inner critic, that voice that tells us we are not good enough.

Healing your inner child involves acknowledging these memories and developing strategies so you can move beyond them. This allows you to gradually and safely get in touch with the wounded parts of your being.

Doing this brings awareness to the wounded part of you without judgment. It is the same action a loving mother would take when trying to understand what her child is going through. Once one understands the nature of one's sufferings, one can develop healthy strategies to address them. To accomplish this, you first need to connect with your inner adult. What is your inner adult? To answer that question, we first need to go back to the inner child.

The subconscious memories of your childhood may continue to play out in your adult life. As an adult, your inner child may still influence some of your thoughts and behaviors. In contrast, your inner adult is that part of you that can think rationally and make thoughtful decisions. It is the part of you that has always existed in you. However, in certain situations, it may become eclipsed by your subconscious memories and absorb your attention.

Uncovering Emotional Wounds

You are not one self but a conglomerate of separate selves, two of which are your inner child and your adult self. Healing comes when we can communicate with these separate selves, which is done through inner dialogue. Before the healing can occur, one must first understand the nature of the wound that needs healing. The following are exercises for conducting an inner dialogue with your inner child.

Exercise 1: Identifying Your Inner Child's Beliefs

1. Think back to a time as a child when you felt hurt or neglected. As you reflect on

this, write down any words that come to you that describe how you felt about the experience:

Example:

- Abandoned

- Helpless

- Angry

- Scared

- Unloved

- Unworthy

_____

_____

_____

_____

_____

_____

_____

_____

_____

_____

_____

_____

_____

_____

_____

2. Think about the statements your parents would frequently make to you and write them down.

Example:

- "Why can't you listen?"

- "Why do you always do that?"

- "Stop being a baby!"

- "You drive me crazy!"

- "Stop your crying!

- "Wait till your father comes home!"

_____

_____

_____

_____

_____

_____

_____

_____

_____

_____

_____

_____

_____

_____

_____

_____

3. Next, reflect on your parents' relationship with each other.

Example:

- They frequently fought.

- They did not talk much to each other.

- My father was domineering and controlling.

- They did not spend much time together.

- There was tension between them.

_____

_____

_____

_____

_____

_____

_____

_____

_____

_____

_____

_____

_____

_____

_____

_____

_____

The previous three steps to this exercise were intended to recall your childhood experience. These experiences may have shaped how you felt about yourself as a child. These experiences played a role in forming your beliefs about yourself.

Use your inner dialogue to connect with your inner child by becoming quiet and paying attention to whatever thoughts come to you. What negative beliefs did your inner child create about themselves based on the previous three steps of this exercise? You can use the following prompts to help you identify these beliefs:

"I am _____."

"I am not_____."

"I cannot_____."

"I will never____."

The following are examples of beliefs:

- I am not a good person.

- I am not worthy.

- I cannot trust anyone.

- I am not lovable.

- I will never be successful in life.

- It is my fault.

- I am stupid.

- I am ugly.

- I cannot do anything right.

- I will never be successful.

Record your beliefs in the space below.

_____

_____

_____

_____

_____

_____

_____

_____

_____

_____

_____

_____

_____

_____

_____

_____

_____

_____

_____

_____

_____

_____

_____

Reflect on what you experienced in doing this exercise, and then answer the following questions:

1. What negative experiences from childhood continue to affect your life today as an adult?

2. How do these experiences impact your life today?

Reflect on these questions and write your response in a journal. When writing, include anything that comes to mind.

By doing this exercise, you will have used your inner voice to connect with your inner child. You will have taken the first step in the healing process: identifying how your inner child impacts your life today.

Releasing Past Traumas

In the last section, you learned how to identify the part of your inner child that needs healing. When you have identified it, the next step is to release past traumas from your mind and body. Regardless of what subconscious memories we may have from childhood, the consequences of those memories will create stress in the body. One approach to healing is to reduce that stress. Fortunately, one of the most powerful stress busters is your breath.

The challenge is that most of us do not breathe properly. We often take shallow breaths instead of deep ones. Shallow breathing is often due to stress. It can start when we are young and become a habit that lasts a lifetime.

A Society of Shallow Breathers

Though breathing occurs involuntarily, we can develop bad habits by repeatedly breathing improperly. Many people have developed the habit of breathing in, holding the air in their chest area, and exhaling. In doing so, the lungs are not fully filled. When breathing properly, the breath should fill the lungs, meaning breathing needs to involve the diaphragm.

The diaphragm draws air into the lungs during inhalation and forces it out during exhalation. When we do not pay attention to our breathing, the air we breathe in remains in the chest area instead. When this occurs, we start depending on the intercostal muscles between the ribs to work harder.

One theory for why we have developed shallow breathing habits is that we live in a society filled with stress. To deal with that stress, we have blocked out many negative emotions. We often hold back our sorrow, pain, or shock. When we hold back our emotions, we also hold back our breath, which becomes irregular. Further, we automatically take shallow breaths when feeling threatened or experiencing strong emotions.

These kinds of responses are expressions of the fight-or-flight response. During such times, our muscles contract, making us tense and affecting our breath. Such breathing patterns can begin early in life and become a habit by adulthood. Shallow breathing can cause stress as a result of the insufficient amount of oxygen flowing through the body. Further, research has shown that this breathing-stress pattern is elevated when browsing through social media.

Researchers theorized that this elevation in the breathing-stress pattern comes from the continuous processing of stressful content. The stressful information brings about tension in the body and shallow breathing. The researchers concluded that stress brings about shallow breathing, while shallow breathing brings about stress. Unless there is a change in breathing habits, these patterns become habitual (Desai, 2020).

Another proposed theory for the ubiquity of shallow breathing patterns has to do with our standards for beauty. In an American culture where slimness is favored, many people—particularly women—suck in their stomachs to improve their physical appearance.

When the abdomen is sucked in, deep breathing is not possible. What happens is that the stomach is sucked in when breathing in and pushed out when exhaling, which is the opposite of correct breathing. When breathing correctly, the belly is filled with air and contracted when exhaling. We can dramatically change our mental and physical well-being by improving our breathing. What is great about using breathing techniques is that they are available to all of us; they are natural and safe.

Mindful Breathing

Everyone can practice mindful breathing due to its simplicity. Mindful breathing means paying attention to one's breath and the sensations that accompany it. When performing mindful breathing, you are not changing how you breathe. Rather you are becoming aware of it.

By bringing your attention to your breathing, you are brought into the present moment instead of being caught up in thought. Mindful breathing is often used in conjunction with different behavioral therapies, including dialectical behavior, cognitive-behavioral, and acceptance and commitment therapies.

How Mindful Breathing Impacts the Mind and Body

Mindful breathing brings about relaxation and improved moods, but how does it do this? The answer to this question lies in the connection that exists between our bodies and emotions.

How we use our bodies affects how we feel emotionally. For example, if you stand straight and hold up your head, you will feel more confident. You will feel less confident if you hold your head down and slump your shoulders. If you smile, you will feel happier than before you smiled. These are just a few examples of how changes in the body affect us emotionally.

If you are in a comfortable situation and feel relaxed, your breathing will slow and deepen. The parasympathetic nervous system creates the effects of relaxation. When stressed or anxious, our breath will be short and shallow. Often, we will breathe through our mouths while not breathing fully. Also, our breath may only reach the top area of our lungs.

The restriction of airflow to the body may lead to feelings of tension and discomfort. In these situations, your breathing affects your mind and body. Also, the triggering of the sympathetic nervous system creates the resulting anxiety.

Mindful breathing techniques lower stress levels by making our breathing intentional. They cause us to breathe deeply and to notice the flow of the in and out breath. Deep breathing fills our lungs, which increases the oxygenation of the body and triggers the body's relaxation state.

The reason why many mindfulness and yoga techniques are effective in inducing relaxation is that they call for us to place our attention on the breath. Placing our attention on the breath induces relaxation and causes us to breathe slower and deeper while shifting our attention away from our thoughts.

Benefits of Mindful Breathing

The benefits of mindful breathing are broad and encompass both the mental and physical realms.

Pain Relief

Mindful breathing is effective in lowering pain levels and intensity. It has been recommended that further studies be conducted to determine if mindful breathing could provide an alternative to opioids for those who suffer from migraines, lower back pain, fibromyalgia, and other chronic pain conditions.

There are reports of mindful breathing being used by patients undergoing cancer treatment. It appears that mindful breathing can lessen symptoms, lessen pain, and reduce the side effects of chemotherapy, such as fatigue, nausea, and anxiety. Mindful breathing also appears to improve immune system functioning (Zeidan & Vago, 2016).

Anxiety Reduction

Mindful breathing exercises have been shown to activate the parasympathetic nervous system while deactivating the sympathetic nervous system. The fight-or-flight response, which is how an organism reacts to a threatening situation, is connected to the sympathetic nervous system.

The parasympathetic nervous system kicks in when the organism no longer feels threatened. Its function is to calm the body and return it to a relaxed state. Blood pressure is lowered, and the heart rate slows down. These actions reduced anxiety levels.

Because of mindful breathing's ability to induce a relaxed state, some believe that it may help reduce job burnout, anxiety, emotional exhaustion, and cynicism (Flook et al., 2013).

Reduced Negativity

Mindful breathing has been demonstrated to reduce negative thinking, which is often associated with individuals experiencing depression. The reduction of negative thinking is accompanied by an improved mood (Zeidan & Vago, 2016).

Diminished Anxiety

Research has demonstrated that mindful breathing is an effective way to manage anxiety. One study demonstrated that students who practiced mindful breathing before taking a test experienced less test anxiety than those who did not practice mindful breathing (Zeidan & Vago, 2016).

Reduction in Depression

Research suggests that mindful breathing techniques can lower depression and PTSD symptoms. It is believed that these benefits are due to the activation of the parasympathetic nervous system (Zeidan & Vago, 2016).

Breathing and the Relaxation Response

To better understand how different breathing techniques create a relaxation response, we can use a breathing technique known as cardiac coherence as an example. Cardiac coherence is a technique for coordinating breathing patterns with one's heart rate. One can stabilize one's heart rate by slowing one's breathing rate.

Cardiac coherence is based on the fact that slow, deep breathing affects the vagus nerve, stabilizing the activity of many internal organs. A sense of calm spreads through the body as the heart rate slows, blood pressure drops, and the muscles relax. In turn, the parasympathetic nervous system informs the brain of these changes, which brings a sense of relaxation to the mind.

The cardiac coherence technique involves inhaling for five seconds and then exhaling for the same length. In other words, the inhalation and exhalation cycle lasts ten seconds. Research using biofeedback machines demonstrates that practicing the cardiac coherence technique results in increased consistency regarding the amount of time between heartbeats. Because of this change in heart rate, there is an anxiety reduction.

But you do not have to do coherence breathing to feel more relaxed. There has been much research to show that we can reduce stress and negative emotions whenever we intentionally place our attention on our breath. The following are the steps to perform mindful breathing:

Mindful Breathing

1. Sit comfortably and close your eyes.

2. Breathe naturally as you focus on the sensations you experience as the air enters and leaves your body.

3. As you breathe in, say to yourself, "Breathing in, I experience calm." As you exhale, say, "Breathing out, I experience calm."

4. Fully experience the sensations as you breathe and focus on your breath's flow. Make the flow of your breath the focus of your attention. Let your breath flow naturally; do not attempt to control it in any way.

5. As you focus on your breath, feel the soothing experience that your breath brings.

6. If you have any concerns, surrender to them by returning your focus to your breath. Take refuge in the inner peace that your breath brings.

7. Maintain your focus on your in and out breath. Make this your anchor point whenever your mind wanders.

8. Whenever worrisome thoughts arise, allow them to appear but return your attention to your breath. Do this repeatedly until the worrisome thought fades away.

Intentional Breathing

When breathing properly, we take deep and full breaths. Doing so relieves stress and brings about a sense of well-being. We breathe correctly when we become intentional in our breathing.

Intentional breathing differs from other breathing techniques described in this book in that the emphasis is on allowing for the natural flow of the breath, which is from the top of the lungs downward during inhalation and from the bottom up during exhalation.

Before attempting intentional breathing, it is important to keep the following in mind:

- Intentional breathing takes practice. For most people, it does not come naturally. This is because most of us do not breathe properly out of habit. Because of this, you may find intentional breathing awkward, strange, or difficult. This kind of reaction is normal. Be patient with yourself and approach intentional breathing as a new learning experience that will take time before you become skillful at it.

- When practicing intentional breathing, do not push yourself. If you feel uncomfortable doing it, take a break from it and try it again later when you feel up to it.

Having said this, the following are the steps to intentional breathing:

1. Find a comfortable place to sit or lie on your back.

2. Place your attention on your breath. Notice how you breathe by observing how your breath flows. Where does the flow of your breath travel? Do you feel it in your upper chest, abdomen, back, front, or sides?

3. Notice the flow of your breath without judging how you are breathing. You may notice that your breathing rate slows down by simply observing your breath.

4. Next, rest your right hand in the center of your chest. More specifically, place it on the sternum, which is located just below the center of your rib cage. Place your left hand on your abdomen, just below your navel.

5. Continue to breathe as you normally do. As you breathe, notice where most of your breathing is taking place. Do you notice it more under your right hand or left hand?

6. As you breathe, take note of how your body feels. What do you notice as you place your attention on your body? Continue to take in your experience for a minimum of 10 breaths.

7. Up until now, you have been instructed to breathe as you normally do. You will now adjust your breathing. Focus on breathing from where your right hand is positioned. Notice how it feels. Do you notice anything different from what you experienced in the previous step?

8. As you continue to breathe from your right hand, see if you can slow down the rate of your inhalations. As you do this, notice how that feels. Continue to do this step for 10–20 breaths. After 10–20 breaths, breathe a few times deeply and then go back to your normal way of breathing.

9. Next, focus on breathing from your left hand, which is positioned on your abdomen. As you do so, notice how breathing feels from this space. Continue to do this step for 10–20 breaths. After 10–20 breaths, breathe a few times deeply and then go back to your normal way of breathing.

10. In this step, you will take half breaths as you go from one hand to the next. First, inhale halfway from your right hand, pause for a second, and then complete your inhalation from your left hand.

11. Pause for a second and reverse the steps by exhaling halfway from your left hand and then completing the exhalation from beneath your right hand.

12. Continue with your next inhalation by breathing from your right hand and letting it flow to your left hand. When exhaling, let it come from your left hand and flow to your right hand. Continue to do this step for 10–20 breaths. After 10–20 breaths, breathe a few times deeply and then go back to your normal way of breathing.

13. Lastly, try to breathe fully and deeply from your right hand as you inhale and from your left hand to your right hand when you exhale. Do so without any pauses. When doing this step, try extending the length of your exhalations so they are of a longer duration than your inhalations. If it is helpful, you can count your breaths to determine if your exhalations are longer than your inhalations. After 10–20 breaths, breathe a few times deeply and then go back to your normal way of breathing.

Notice how you are feeling after the last step. Did you find this exercise difficult? Did breathing fully and slowly seem strange to you? How do you feel emotionally and physically? What about your level of energy? Notice all these things. Intentional breathing takes practice, but it can become second nature to you with enough practice.

As mentioned before, most of us do not breathe properly, which is why we often feel stressed. Intentional breathing represents the proper way to breathe. It involves taking full breaths and breathing from the top down during inhalations and from the bottom up during exhalations. With continued practice, you will experience the mental, emotional, and physical benefits of taking full, deep, and slow breaths.

Besides mindful and intentional breathing, there are other breathing techniques that can help you manage stress and bring about calmness. This can lead to greater awareness of the thoughts and emotions we are experiencing, which further helps you connect with your inner child. The following are other breathing techniques:

4-7-8 Breathing

When first learning 4-7-8 breathing, it is advisable to practice at least twice a day. Additionally, you should only do four cycles of breathing per day until you become used to this technique. It is normal to feel lightheaded when first practicing this exercise.

1. Sit in a comfortable position while sitting straight.

2. Place your tongue so it is pressed against the back of your upper teeth.

3. Exhale fully from your mouth, allowing the air to flow around your tongue.

4. Inhale through your nose while keeping your mouth closed. Inhale for a count of four.

5. Hold your breath for a seven count.

6. Exhale through the mouth for a count of eight. You may experience a whooshing sound when doing this. Doing this completes one cycle.

7. Repeat for three additional cycles.

Basic Diaphragm Breathing

When first learning this breathing technique, you should perform it while lying on the floor.

1. Get into a relaxed position with your shoulders sinking downward.

2. Place one hand on your chest and the other on your abdomen.

3. Breathing normally, inhale through your nose until you cannot take in any more air.

4. Focus on your breath as it travels from your nostrils to your abdomen. Try to keep chest movement to a minimum.

5. Notice the way your abdomen rises and the sensations you experience.

6. Pull your lips inward as if you were drinking through a straw and exhale. When exhaling, do so slowly for four seconds as your abdomen contracts.

7. Repeat these steps several times.

Besides breathing techniques, meditation is also an effective way to release past traumas. Meditation is the topic of the next section.

Meditation

Meditation is another effective technique for releasing past trauma. It offers major benefits to well-being:

Cultivate Compassion

Meditation expands one's awareness while providing greater clarity about one's experiences. When this occurs, a greater capacity for compassion is formed. This is particularly true for Metta meditation, which we will discuss in this chapter. By repeating compassionate phrases to yourself, you will develop greater self-compassion.

When you develop greater self-compassion, you will be able to reduce the effects of negative emotions such as feelings of:

- Self-doubt

- Unworthiness

- Judgment

- Anger

- Self-criticism

A study demonstrated that meditation was effective in increasing self-compassion in individuals who have post-traumatic stress disorder (Orentas, 2021).

Reduce Anxiety and Stress

Meditation has been shown to reduce stress and anxiety. As your self-compassion grows, you will start to develop a more positive view of yourself. Developing a more positive view of yourself will lead to experiencing positive emotions more frequently. The emotions of love and gratitude have been shown to reduce anxiety and stress.

Pain Reduction

Research has shown that meditation can reduce pain levels in some physical conditions. In the study, it was found that participants who suffered from lower back pain and migraine headaches were able to reduce their level of pain through meditation. The researchers concluded that emotional stress aggravates physical pain, so reducing stress reduced their experience of pain (Carson et al., 2005).

Longer Life

Telomeres are structures located on chromosomes; they protect genetic information. Telomeres grow shorter with age, which causes the body to age. Chronic stress can speed up the aging process. Meditation has been shown to slow down the aging process (Hoge, 2013).

Strengthen Social Connections

Certain meditations, such as Metta meditation, involve reciting phrases to yourself. These phrases are self-affirming and may lead to you becoming kinder and more compassionate to yourself. The kindness and compassion that you offer yourself will cause you to extend them to others, which strengthens social connections.

Become Less Reactive

When one learns to meditate, one changes how one relates to thoughts and emotions. Normally, we identify with or personalize our thoughts and emotions. In other words, if I have a worrisome thought, I tell myself I am worried. If I feel anger, I tell myself that I am angry.

Meditation allows you to calm your mind. In calming your mind, you develop greater awareness of your thoughts and emotions. You can sense them coming and going. However, the difference is that you begin to lose identification with them. Instead of personalizing them, you learn to observe them.

Being able to do this brings about an attitude of acceptance; you no longer resist your thoughts and emotions. This attitude of acceptance allows your inner child to express itself, which brings about healing freely.

Suggestions When Meditating

Many people have trouble meditating. The following are suggestions to help you:

- Be patient with yourself: The ability to meditate takes time and practice.

- Let go of expectations: When meditating, do not have any expectations of what should or should not be happening.

- Do not judge: Do not judge anything that you experience.

- Be willing to experiment: Try meditating in different places, at different times, and with different environments (i.e., music playing, incense, or photographs of people you love).

The following are different meditations for healing your inner child:

Appreciation Meditation

1. Sit down in a comfortable position and close your eyes.

2. Now breathe deeply, hold your breath briefly, then exhale.

3. Follow your breath during inhalation and exhalation. Place your attention on your breath. Feel it as it courses through your body.

4. Think of someone or something you love. As you think of your subject, think of the reasons why you appreciate them. Fully experience your feelings.

5. As you experience these energies, intensify them by employing your other senses, such as touch, hearing, smelling, and taste. To do this, add these other sensory dimensions to your mind's representation of your subject.

    Example: If I am thinking of my spouse, I would also imagine her touching me, hearing her voice, smelling her perfume, and tasting her kiss.

6. By engaging your other senses, the feelings of appreciation will be experienced more deeply.

7. Next, think of a person for whom you have neutral feelings. For example, it could be the store clerk where you do your shopping or the person who delivers your mail.

8. Think about what you can appreciate about this person.

9. As before, fully experience the feelings you are having and try to intensify them.

10. Now, think of someone who irritates you.

11. Think about what you can appreciate about them.

12. Fully experience the feelings you are having and try to intensify them.

13. Now, think of someone you hate.

14. What can you appreciate about them?

15. Fully experience the feelings you are having and try to intensify them.

16. Now, think about yourself. What can you appreciate about yourself?

17. Fully experience the feelings you are having and try to intensify them.

This is the end of this exercise.

The level of your appreciation has less to do with the world around you than it does with your ability to take charge of your energy level. Emotional mastery is the ability to generate appreciation for any experience you may have.

Metta Meditation

In the Pali language, the word "Metta" translates to positive energy or kindness. For this reason, this meditation is also known as the "loving-kindness" meditation. The purpose of Metta meditation is to develop positive emotions toward all living beings. Such emotions would include compassion, gratitude, appreciation, and love.

For inner child work, recite positive phrases to yourself and those from whom you wish to release your hurt or anger. The following are examples of phrases you can repeat:

- May I be peaceful, free of suffering, and safe.

- May I be healthy. May I be happy.

- May I be confident and strong.

When repeating your phrase, it is important that you do it mindfully. Focus on the phrase and the emotions that you experience. The Metta meditation can be performed anywhere. To do it, do the following:

1. Find a comfortable place to sit and close your eyes.

2. Take a deep, slow breath through your nose and then continue to breathe deeply.

3. Pay attention to your breath. Feel the sensations created by your breath as it travels through your body.

4. Focus on your heart and then silently recite your phrase to yourself.

5. As you repeat the phrase, recognize the meaning of the phrase and the way that it makes you feel. Continue to repeat the phrase.

6. Next, think about someone you know and recite the phrase to them. As before, recognize the meaning of the phrase and focus on how it makes you feel.

7. Then think about someone who is an acquaintance or someone you do not know well. Recite the phrase to them. As before, recognize the meaning of the phrase and focus on how it makes you feel.

8. Finally, think about someone who is difficult to get along with. Recite the phrase to them. As before, recognize the meaning of the phrase and focus on how it makes you feel.

When doing this meditation, you can also employ visualization. You can visualize your breath flowing through you, your heart, or the person you are thinking of.

Also, you can change your phrases while doing this meditation.

Gratitude Meditation

1. Sit down in a comfortable position.

2. With your eyes closed, place your attention on your breath as you breathe normally.

3. Focus on the sensations you experience as your breath enters your body during

inhalation and leaves it during exhalation.

4. Be open to everything you experience without any form of judgment or resistance. Greet every experience with complete acceptance.

5. Whenever you find yourself distracted, gently return your awareness to your breath.

6. Everything you experience is an opportunity to express gratitude:

    - You can experience gratitude for a person, a pet, or nature.

    - You can express gratitude for the challenges you have experienced and what you gained from them.

    - You can express gratitude for being alive.

7. When you find yourself experiencing gratitude, try to intensify that feeling. Place your awareness on the feeling of gratitude. What happens when you focus on the emotion of gratitude? You can use this technique to intensify any emotion or feeling you experience.

8. Allow yourself to experience the emotion of gratitude as deeply as possible.

9. If you have trouble with this exercise, keep practicing this meditation until you experience the level of gratitude you desire.

In addition to breathing techniques and meditation, another way to work on inner healing is through journaling, which is the topic of the next section.

Journaling

Journaling is another effective way of releasing trauma. By writing about what you are thinking and feeling, you are drawing them out of yourself and externalizing them. In other words, you are bringing them out into the light of your awareness. When you externalize your thoughts and feelings, they lose their potency, which brings about healing.

Each day, write about what you are thinking and feeling. You can also write from the perspective of your inner child. Inquire with your inner child about what they are experiencing and what they may need from you.

Chapter Writing Prompts

Inner child writing prompts can be a powerful way to access your subconscious mind and connect with your inner child. When a writing prompt asks you to write from the child's viewpoint, try your best to step out of your adult mindset and try to perceive the situation through the child's eyes.

When you have accessed your childhood mindset, write down any memories you have of the events that occurred at that age. Also, write down any emotions you remember experiencing that were associated with those events.

When writing, do not think about it too much. Instead, write down whatever comes to mind. Let your writing flow as thoughts appear. By doing this, you will gain insight into your inner child's pain.

Choose from the writing prompts below and respond to them in your journal.

1. What mistakes did you make as a child that still affect you? How could you begin to practice forgiveness for yourself and let go of your guilt or shame?

2. What are the ways that your inner child experienced abandonment? What could you do to address your inner child's pain and make it feel safe?

3. What critical comments were made to you when you were a child? How did these comments affect your self-image? How could you reframe those comments so that they support you in your healing?

4. What situations trigger you as an adult? Those situations are triggering your wounded inner child. What could you do to address those triggers or situations so that they support you in healing?

5. How did the dynamics of your family affect your inner child? What could you do to address and heal those patterns of thinking or feeling?

6. Connecting with nature has a healing and grounding effect. How could you use nature to heal your inner child and promote your growth?

7. What are ways that you can start letting go of the need to control things so that your inner child can feel more secure and supported?

8. What are your inner child's passions? What could you do to support and nurture those passions?

9. What losses did your inner child experience? What could you do to grieve those losses and heal them?

10. Did your inner child experience traumatic events? What could you do to address those memories and heal them?

11. How can you bring balance to your life so that you can support your inner child's healing?

12. What can you do to address and heal the shame that your inner child experienced?

13. Your imperfections are not negative. Rather, they serve a positive function and indicate an opportunity for further growth. What can you do to teach your inner child that it is okay to make mistakes?

14. Seeking professional support can be valuable for healing your inner child. What can you do to seek professional help? If you are resistant to seeking professional support, why is that? What has it cost you to think that way?

15. Spiritual practices can be invaluable in inner child healing. What can you do to learn about the various spiritual teachings? How can you incorporate those practices into your life to heal the inner child?

16. What rituals or routines can you adopt to nourish and support the well-being of your inner child?

17. How could you incorporate mindfulness into your life for the purpose of creating a deeper connection with your inner child?

CHAPTER 4

Reconnecting with Authenticity

In Chapter 1, you learned how to understand your inner child. In Chapter 2, you learned how to nurture your child. Chapter 3 addressed how to heal emotional wounds. In this chapter, you will learn how to reconnect with your authentic self.

Connecting with and healing your inner child means integrating it with your conscious self. In other words, you are losing the fragmentation that occurs when you continue to suppress this aspect of yourself.

As you integrate your unconscious aspects with your conscious self, you bring forth your authentic self. Your authentic self refers to the state of awareness where you embrace every aspect of who you are.

Embracing Your True Self

Being authentic involves reflecting on your past decisions and seeing how they align with what feels right for you. We frequently compromise our feelings to meet the expectations of others or societal norms.

Your authentic self is the essential you; it is the truth of who you are. It is about doing what feels right for you and following your passion. When you are authentic, you live in a way that gives you peace of mind.

Exercise 1: Life Balance Sheet

Directions: In this exercise, you will reflect on your childhood perspective and compare it to your life today. To prepare for the exercise, get a piece of writing paper and fold it in half lengthwise to form two columns. Also, get a second sheet of paper, which you will not need to fold.

1. Take a moment to relax and close your eyes.

2. Think back to your earliest memories as a child. As you do, think about the following questions. When you get an answer, write your response on the left-hand side of the paper:

   a) As a child, what did you want to be when you grew up?

   b) What was your earliest memory of being happy?

   c) Regarding this memory, what were you doing at that moment?

   d) Were there others with you at this time? If so, who were they?

   e) How were you feeling at that time? How right did that moment feel to you? Rate that feeling on a scale of 0–10, with 10 being the highest.

3. Next, use the right side of the paper to respond to the following questions:

   a) As an adult, what are you doing today?

   b) Did anyone influence your decision to go into your line of work? If so, who?

   c) Did your current job turn out to be what you expected it to be?

   d) Were there aspects of your personality that were enhanced by getting into your line of work?

   e) What is the story you tell yourself as to why you entered your current position?

f) Did you choose your position, or did your career choose you?

4. Next, get the second sheet of paper and answer the following questions:

   a) Think about when you were happy most recently. What were you doing at that moment?

   b) Was there anyone with you at that time? If so, who were they?

   c) Were you feeling any other emotions besides happiness?

   d) How right did that moment feel to you? Rate that feeling on a scale of 0-10, with 10 being the highest.

   e) Has the way you experience happiness changed for you since you were a child?

   f) Do you feel like you are being true to yourself? Do you feel that you are being your authentic self?

   g) In what parts of your life do you feel you can express your authentic self? Is it a relationship, your job, or an area of interest?

5. Next, take the first paper and review your responses. As you do so, answer the following questions:

   a) Do any of your responses regarding your past align with your current life? Example: Did anything that brought you happiness as a child get carried over to today?

   b) Do you find anything on the first paper that catches your attention?

   c) As for what you wanted to be when you grew up, does it align with what you are doing today? If not, what happened?

6. Finally, compare your first sheet of paper with the second one and answer the following questions:

a) Where do you see any alignment? Where do you see any disconnects?

b) There were aspects of your childhood where you felt you could be your authentic self. Did any of these aspects remain with you over time?

c) What aspects of your authentic self were left behind?

d) What stands out to you the most after doing this exercise?

e) Do you plan to do anything about it?

It is important to note that living authentically does not necessarily mean doing what you are passionate about. Living authentically sometimes means doing what works for you.

Let's say you have a job that meets your financial needs. Though you would rather be doing something you are passionate about, you need to take care of your family. As long as you know this, you are being authentic. It is a problem when you are unaware of what is authentic for you and continue to go against it.

The most important thing is that you live your life in a way that makes sense to you. This requires that you be aware of what feels authentic to you and do your best to live your life accordingly.

Expressing Suppressed Emotions and Desires

As stated earlier, the inner child holds the memories from childhood that are suppressed. However, childhood memories are not the only things that are suppressed. We often also suppress our emotions, desires, and needs. To become authentic, we need to get in touch with and embrace all these things.

Being able to experience and express your emotions is of great importance for developing healthy relationships with yourself and others. The reason for this is that emotions serve the following functions:

- They help us understand ourselves by informing us of what we are experiencing. Example: Does a certain situation bring about feelings of happiness or fear?

- Emotions help us understand others by showing us what they are experiencing.

- Emotions help us in decision-making by informing us of what we are experiencing.

- Emotions help us understand our desires and needs.

The following are exercises for getting in touch with your authentic self:

Exercise 2: A Letter from the Self

Directions: Write a letter to yourself expressing your deepest desires and aspirations. As you write the letter, get in touch with the feelings you experience.

Exercise 3: A Letter of Open Dialogue

Directions: In this exercise, you will conduct an open dialogue with your inner child through letter form:

Take a moment to think back to your childhood memories but from an adult perspective. Provide insights or your adult explanations for troubling situations that, at the time, you did not understand.

By sharing your understanding with your inner child, you can help them make sense of those situations, thus allowing them to begin healing.

You can also write to your inner child to offer reassurance, comfort, and hope. As you write, ask your inner child questions such as:

- How does that make you feel?

- What can I do to support you?

- What do you need for me?

When asking these questions, take time to sit with them and allow the answers to come to you. Do not look for the answers.

Exercise 4: Creative Release

Directions: Engage in a creative activity that will allow you to express your emotions. Examples of such creative activities include:

- Drawing

- Painting

- Sculpting

- Dancing

- Music

- Writing

Exercise 5: Meditation for Observing Emotions

Directions: This meditation will allow you to explore your emotions without getting caught up in them.

1. Get into a comfortable position and close your eyes.

2. Place your attention on your breath. Notice the sensations that you experience as you breathe. Continue to do so until you feel relaxed.

3. Whenever you become distracted by thoughts, return your attention to your breath.

4. Place your attention on any emotions that you may be experiencing. Emotions can feel positive, neutral, or negative. Give your complete acceptance of whatever emotion you may be experiencing. Do not try to change it or dismiss it.

5. Stay with the feeling of the emotion. Make it the focus of your attention.

6. Notice that you are the observer of the emotion. Be aware of it but not caught up in it.

7. Stay with the emotion for as long as you wish. Notice that no emotion can harm you when you observe it.

Chapter Writing Prompts

Inner child writing prompts can be a powerful way to access your subconscious mind and connect with your inner child. When writing, do not think about it too much. Instead, write down whatever comes to mind. Let your writing flow as thoughts appear. By doing this, you will gain insight into your inner child's pain.

Choose from the writing prompts below and respond to them in your journal.

1. If you could go back in time and talk to your childhood self, what single piece of advice would you give them?

2. If you could go back in time and talk to your high school self, what single piece of advice would you give them?

3. Think about a day in your life from five years ago and then compare it to today. Has your life changed? If so, how has it changed? Is it a change for the better?

4. Imagine in your mind your happiest place. Where is this place? What do you see, smell, hear, and feel? What makes this place special to you? What can you do to recreate this place where you are now?

5. Imagine working at your dream job. What are you doing? Where are you? What does your workday look like? What is preventing you from making this your real job?

6. When do you feel like you are being your most authentic self? Why do you think that is? What is preventing you from being that way more often?

7. What activities do you feel allow you to express your inner child? Why do you think that is? What can you do to experience that more frequently?

8. What is your biggest fear? Why is that?

9. What is it about you that makes you unique?

10. Select ten things about yourself that you love.

CHAPTER 5

Reparenting Your Inner Child

In Chapter 1, you learned how to understand your inner child. In Chapter 2, you learned to nurture your child. Chapter 3 addressed how to heal emotional wounds. In Chapter 4, you learned how to reconnect with your authentic self. In this chapter, you will learn how to reparent your inner child.

Before you started inner child work, your inner child had remained abandoned. Without any adult guidance, it was allowed to remain fearful. In the previous chapters of this workbook, you brought awareness to your inner child, connected with it, gained its trust, and worked on nurturing it. Now it is time to take charge of your inner child by letting it know that it no longer has to fend for itself. It is time to show your inner child that it no longer has to be afraid.

Becoming a Nurturing Parent to Your Inner Child

Reparenting your inner child involves learning how to care for yourself. It involves detecting the old patterns of thinking and feeling that your inner child drove and then replacing them with ones that support you in feeling whole.

The essence of reparenting is learning to deal with your thoughts and emotions responsibly but compassionately. For example, the next time you feel triggered, acknowledge the feeling of being triggered and ask yourself, "What can I do to soothe myself?" or "What can I do to make myself feel safe?" By communicating with yourself compassionately and with nurture, you are practicing self-parenting.

Affirmations

One way of developing a positive internal dialogue with yourself is to use affirmations. Affirmations are words of empowerment that you say to yourself. By repeating your affirmations enough times, you will create a new way of thinking. The following are things to remember when using affirmations:

Repetition

Habits are created when we repeat a behavior over a period of time, usually between one and three months. When first repeating affirmations, it may seem like nothing is happening. This is normal, so stick with it.

The greater the repetition, the more ingrained your affirmation will become in your mind. It takes about a month of repetition before you experience notable changes in how you think and feel.

Emotion

When you are repeating your affirmations, evoke emotion. Repeat your affirmations with a sense of certainty as though their words are your current reality. Also, select affirmations that resonate with you. Repeating affirmations is ineffective if you do not believe what you are saying.

If, when repeating an affirmation, you feel a sense of calm or relief, you have chosen the right affirmation. Also, affirmations are more effective when repeated out loud.

Daily Affirmations

Directions: Select from the following affirmations that resonate with you. Select your favorite ones and recite them three times daily. When reciting them, be sure to express them with emotion. Do this for thirty days.

My life is a gift for me to discover and unwrap.

I am loved by the universe, and all my experiences are for my pruning.

I proudly express my beliefs and what I stand for.

I am proud and beautiful.

My dignity and worth as a human being are granted by my creator.

I am worthy of respect.

I am intelligent and wise.

I am intelligent and capable.

I am worthy because I exist.

I am loved. I give love. I am love.

I deserve all the good things that come to me.

I take time for self-care because I am worth it.

I honor myself by being true to who I am.

I have something to give to this world.

I celebrate life for giving me life.

I am a good person, and I am worthy.

I am a source of love, strength, and faith.

I honor and believe in myself.

My happiness is deserved because I exist.

I am more than enough to be successful.

I am good enough just being me.

I am worthy of respect and dignity.

I am worthy of appreciation.

I love myself for who I am.

I forgive others.

I am worthy of success.

I am committed to achieving my dreams.

I forgive myself.

I am committed to my success.

I am blessed with love.

I am blessed with faith and hope.

I embrace love.

I forgive the past and embrace the future.

I am blessed with hidden talents.

In the art of life, I am a masterpiece.

I have everything I need.

I am prosperous in heart and spirit.

I am proud of who I am.

I love myself just the way I am.

I am grateful for all my life's experiences.

I am worthy; I deserve all the good things that come to me.

I am a loving and supportive friend.

I am healthy, strong, and beautiful.

My strength is in my vulnerability.

I am loved and supported by the universe.

My self-worth is without conditions.

I honor my feelings, for they are valid.

I heal myself by allowing myself to experience all that I feel.

I come closer to healing whenever I embrace my inner child.

I will achieve my dream life by taking full responsibility for my life.

I give my peace of mind the highest priority.

I allow myself to say "No" without guilt.

I am worthy of respect and of giving respect.

It is by acknowledging my pain that I begin the process of healing.

I let go of guilt and embrace forgiveness for myself and others.

I and I alone determine how I want to be and live.

My personal happiness is more important than the expectations of others.

I celebrate my small victories.

I have faith in the person I am.

I am good enough, just as I am.

I honor my hopes and dreams.

Life loves me, and I love life.

I celebrate my progress in becoming a better person.

I accept myself for who I am because that is the way to victory.

Besides affirmations, there are other ways that you can become a nurturing parent to your inner child. They include the following:

Create a Self-Parenting Vision Board

Directions: Get a poster board and attach images, words, and affirmations that remind you of how you want to treat yourself. When completed, hang the vision board where you will see it daily.

Create a Self-Care List

Directions: Make a list of activities you can engage in that soothe and comfort you. Include activities like being in nature, meditating, taking a hot bath, and so on. Always keep the list with you. Whenever you experience negative thoughts about yourself, engage in one of the items on your list.

Setting boundaries is an important part of caring for your inner child. Setting boundaries is the subject of the next section.

Setting Boundaries

What comes to mind when you hear the word "boundaries"? For many, this word

brings thoughts of keeping others at a distance or rigidness. With a better understanding of boundary setting, I believe that you will find a more empowering meaning, such as liberation and self-empowerment.

Rather than creating distance or building walls, setting boundaries demonstrates self-respect, growth, and peace of mind. Boundaries are rules that you make for yourself to keep you feeling safe when engaging with others. In doing so, you are demonstrating self-love.

When you create boundaries and communicate them to others, you are creating an environment where you can feel safe while letting others know of your needs. Doing this can help minimize misunderstandings or arguments.

Since you create your boundaries so that you can feel safe, you can be flexible with them. As your relationships with others evolve, you can adjust your boundaries as you see fit. Boundaries should be created for any kind of relationship, as setting boundaries lets others know how you want to be treated.

Why Boundaries Are Important

Imagine that you and another person are playing a game, but they do not know what the rules are. Not knowing the rules, this person makes a move that is not allowed. You then must correct them and explain to them that they cannot do that. How were they supposed to know that if they did not know what the rules were?

When it comes to setting boundaries, it can get more complicated. Many of us do not know our own rules! Someone may do something that makes us uncomfortable. In response, we may become reactive and get caught up in our emotions. When we are in this state, we may not be clear as to why we feel the way we do. By setting boundaries, you will know what your needs are and be able to communicate them to others. In turn, they will know what you expect from them.

Creating Your Boundaries

Besides becoming a nurturing parent to yourself, it is just as important to set boundaries for yourself and find ways to get your emotional needs met. It is important that you let others know what your boundaries are and that you enforce them.

If you need to be alone when you are feeling conflict with another person, you need to communicate that to them. If others do not respect your boundaries, you must let them know of the consequences should they continue to not honor them.

When setting boundaries, you must be consistent with them. In other words, do not compromise your boundaries unless you feel that you are emotionally safe. Also, it is important that you are respectful of others when imposing your boundaries on them.

Now that you understand what personal boundaries are, it is time for you to create them. The following are two exercises for creating your boundaries.

Exercise 1: Create a Plan for Your Boundaries

Directions: Create a list of areas in your life where you need to create boundaries. Remember, boundaries are intended to keep you feeling emotionally safe. For example, you may need boundaries when others discuss certain subjects you are uncomfortable with.

When you create your list of areas, define your boundaries for those areas. If you need others not to judge you when you share your concerns with them, your boundary might be something like, "When I share my concerns with you, I need you to respect how I feel."

The following are some additional examples:

- "When we are with each other, it is important to me that you do not talk about _____."

- "When I tell you that I need to be alone, I need you to respect that."

- "If you are going to be late, I need you to call me."

Related to setting boundaries is learning to meet our emotional needs. Sometimes we may develop codependency with others to meet our emotional needs. Someone may depend on a relationship to feel secure or needed. When this occurs, our emotional well-being is dependent on whether others are there for us.

True happiness can only come when we learn to take charge of meeting our emotional needs. Instead of waiting for someone else to make us feel secure or needed, we can find ways to experience these feelings on our own. This brings us to the importance of knowing what our values are.

Values

To become the best version of ourselves, we must learn to live by our values. Anytime we live in a manner inconsistent with our values, we create resistance in our lives. If your life is not aligned with your values, start the process of making changes in your life so that you can start moving toward greater alignment.

If you currently have a job that conflicts with your values, what can you do to create the needed changes in your work? Could you conduct your work differently? Would it require you to take on a different position? Perhaps it means finding a new job. If your relationship does not align with your values, what changes do you need to make? Do you need to transform your relationship or find a new one?

Consider any aspect of your life where you experience a gap between how you live your life and the values you hold. For you to set boundaries for yourself, you first need to know what your values are. When asked what they value, people will often say things like family, country, friendship, or honesty.

For the sake of this book, values refer to the emotions or feelings that we want to experience. For example, someone may say that they value family. If you ask them why they value family, they may say that they value the feeling of connection that comes with being part of a family. In this example, what the person is really valuing is the feeling of connection. Family is a way for them to experience that feeling. In the following exercise, you learn how to identify your top values.

Exercise 2: Values

Part 1: Identify Your Values

Get your journal or a piece of paper and write down what you value. In other words, what are the feelings that you want to experience? This first part of the exercise is a brainstorming session, so just write whatever comes to mind. The following are examples of values (feelings or emotional states):

- Respected

- Happiness

- Adventure

- Significance

- Playfulness

- Excitement

- Peaceful

- Connection

After reviewing your list, choose the values that are most important to you. You can do this by asking yourself, "If I could only choose one value to experience, which one would it be?" Using the previous example, let us say that value is feeling respected. Write the number "1" by "respected." Go to the next value, which is happiness. Ask yourself the question again: "If I could only choose one value to experience, which one would it be?"

Look at the rest of your list. If happiness is more important to you than any remaining items, write the number 2 by "happiness." If you find another item more important to you than happiness, write "2" by that item.

Continue with this process for each item on your list until you have your top ten values. **Example**: "Adventure" is the next item on the list. You would check to see if any of the remaining items on the list are more important than "adventure. "You would write a "3" by that item.

Chapter Writing Prompts

Inner child writing prompts can be a powerful way to access your subconscious mind and connect with your inner child. When a writing prompt asks you to write from the child's viewpoint, try your best to step out of your adult mindset and try to perceive the situation through the child's eyes.

When you have accessed your childhood mindset, write down any memories you have of the events that occurred at that age. Also, write down any emotions you remember experiencing that were associated with those events.

When writing, do not think about it too much. Instead, write down whatever comes to mind. Let your writing flow as thoughts appear. By doing this, you will gain insight into your inner child's pain.

Choose from the writing prompts below and respond to them in your journal.

1. How can you become more self-compassionate toward yourself? How could you show more kindness toward your inner child?

2. What anger is your inner child holding on to? What can you do to release that anger and create an opportunity for growth and healing?

3. As a child, how were your emotions invalidated? What can you do to validate your emotions and support your inner child's?

4. What can you do to regain the trust of your inner child? What actions can you take to build a trusting relationship?

5. As a child, was your voice silenced? What could you do today to encourage your inner child to express themselves?

6. How can you demonstrate understanding and patience for your inner child so that it can heal?

7. What could you do to become more vulnerable and demonstrate to your inner child that it is safe for it to express itself and be authentic?

8. What needs went unmet when you were a child? What can you do today to start fulfilling those needs?

9. What are your inner child's fears? Do you retain those fears within you today? What could you do to address them and overcome them?

10. What can you do to reparent your inner child and provide it with the love, support, and guidance that it needs?

11. How could you begin to embrace change while supporting your inner child through life's changes?

12. What can you do to become more resilient? What can you do to assist your inner child in overcoming challenges or setbacks?

13. What can you do to set healthy boundaries that will empower you and help heal your inner child? How can you start practicing saying "No"?

14. What are the unique characteristics of your inner child? What can you do to celebrate and honor those qualities?

15. Your intuition is a product of your inner child. What could you do to honor your intuition and its guidance?

16. What can you do to bring more playfulness and joy into your life?

17. How could you use creative pursuits to bring about healing for your inner child?

18. What achievements did you have as a child that deserve celebrating?

19. As a child, what were your dreams? What could you do today to honor those dreams and pursue them?

20. Life is about continuous growth. What can you do to cultivate a growth mindset? What can you do to teach your inner child that they can grow?

CHAPTER 6

Forgiveness, Compassion, and Letting Go

Forgiveness, compassion, and letting go of the past are the essence of healing the inner child. Further, these three qualities are interrelated. In this chapter, you will learn how to cultivate all three.

Forgiveness

The importance of being able to forgive is widely extolled by spiritual teachings and mental health experts. The reason for this is simple. Being able to forgive offers powerful benefits. On the other hand, holding on to resentments and grudges may lead to complications in our lives. It can affect our relationships as well as our emotional and physical health.

Numerous studies have linked holding on to resentment with higher risks of heart disease, increased blood pressure, and cognitive decline.

What Does It Mean to Forgive?

Many people find it difficult to forgive, whether it is forgiving themselves or others. One reason for this may be a misunderstanding of what forgiveness is. Forgiveness means choosing to make peace with the past as opposed to holding on to the need to receive an apology or seek revenge. More specifically:

- Forgiveness does not mean condoning or excusing past offenses by others or ourselves.

- Forgiveness does not mean forgetting about what happened in the past.

- Forgiveness does not mean tolerating what was done to us or what we did to others.

- Forgiveness does not mean you need to trust those who have harmed you in the past.

Instead, forgiveness is about purging ourselves from anger and resentment, which are toxic when we hold on to them. While learning to forgive is not easy, it is well worth it. Also, learning to forgive takes time, and it occurs in incremental steps. For this reason, it is important to be patient with yourself and learn to let go at your own pace.

The Benefits of Forgiving

When we learn to forgive, a powerful transformation occurs. When you have been harmed by another, holding on to negative emotions such as resentment or anger can feel like they have power over us. It is a toxicity that eats away at us both emotionally and physically.

When we learn to forgive, we reclaim our power over the offense that was committed against us. The following are some of the benefits of forgiveness:

- Enhanced mental health

- Enhanced quality of life

- Enhanced self-esteem

- Reduction in stress levels

- Reduction in negative emotions

- Improved quality of sleep and eating habits.

In addition to these general benefits, forgiveness also offers specific benefits to the healing process:

The Deliverer of Peace

Being able to forgive will deliver peace to your life and the lives of others. When you forgive, it invites peace into your life while, at the same time, it may help others with their self-esteem. The reason for this is that no one is perfect; everyone makes mistakes.

Sometimes, when we are offended, we forget this and express our hostility to the other person. When we forgive others, they are more likely to forgive themselves.

Taking Back Your Power

When we experience trauma from the actions of others, the harm that is inflicted on us is compounded by our own patterns of self-defeating thoughts or behaviors. When we learn to forgive, we can take back control of our lives.

Improve Your Connections with People

When we hold anger and resentment toward another, it not only affects our relationship with them. Our holding on to these negative emotions will also affect our connection with all our relationships. It may show up as having a short temper or trust issues. By offering forgiveness, we can strengthen those connections.

Forgiveness and Reconciliation

There are some with whom we may not wish to reconcile as we may believe that the relationship is not worth it. However, there are relationships that are worth reconciling. Forgiveness makes that possible.

How to Begin Forgiving

How do you start the process of forgiving? What happens when the one you need to forgive is yourself? How do you begin the process of forgiving yourself? The following exercises will show you how.

Exercise 1: The Forgiveness Meditation

The forgiveness meditation can be used to start the forgiveness process, whether the person you want to forgive is someone else or yourself.

1. Sit in a comfortable position and close your eyes.

2. As you sit, breathe naturally. Let your mind and body relax.

3. Place your attention on the area of your heart. Notice the sensations that you feel there. When we do not forgive, we harbor anger or resentment. The energy of these emotions fills our bodies, in particular the heart area. It may appear as a hard, restrictive, or numb sensation.

4. Feel the pain that comes from having your heart closed.

5. Breathe softly and start offering forgiveness or giving it to yourself.

The following are statements of forgiveness. Choose the one that is relevant to you and recite it. As you recite the forgiveness statement, allow any feelings or images that may arise to present themselves to you. Have total acceptance of them. You can repeat the statements as often as you wish.

The following are the statements:

Asking for Forgiveness for Harming Others

Recite the following:

During my lifetime, I have caused harm to many. I have done so knowingly and unknowingly. I have done so out of my own pain, anger, fear, or confusion.

As you recite this statement, recall the ways that you have hurt others. Try to visualize these situations in your mind. As you do so, feel the pain, regret, or sorrow that is within you.

When you are ready, release yourself from this burden and ask for forgiveness. For each memory of you causing hurt to another, ask for forgiveness.

Forgiving Yourself

Recite the following:

There are many ways that I have harmed or hurt myself. Many times, I have abandoned or betrayed myself. I have done so knowingly and unknowingly through my thoughts, actions, or words.

After reading this, get in touch with how precious your body and life are.

1. In your mind, see the ways that you have caused harm to yourself. Try to visualize these situations in your mind.

2. Get in touch with the sorrow that you have been carrying within you, knowing that you can release it when you are ready.

3. For each instance that you remember causing harm to yourself, extend forgiveness to yourself.

4. Repeat the following: *For all the ways that I hurt myself through my actions or inactions or out of my pain, fear, or confusion, I now offer sincere forgiveness to myself.*

Forgiveness for Those Who Harmed You

Recite the following:

There have been numerous ways that I have been hurt, abandoned, or abused. Others have done to me knowingly or unknowingly through their thoughts, actions, or words.

In your mind, see the many ways that you have been harmed. As you do so, feel the pain that you have been carrying all this time and realize that you can release this burden when you are ready.

Next, say the following to yourself:

I now recall the many ways that I have been harmed by others. They have done so through their own pain, fear, confusion, or anger. I have carried this burden within me for too long. To the best of my abilities at this moment, I offer forgiveness to all those who have harmed me. I forgive you.

Continue to repeat these three statements until you feel the weight from your heart lifted. For pains that are deeper, you may not experience any release. If this is true for you, know that this is okay. Offering forgiveness cannot be forced. It can only occur when you are ready to move on.

Continue to perform these meditations and allow the images in your mind and the words from the three statements to work their way into your mind. You can make the forgiveness meditation part of your daily routine.

Embracing Self-Compassion

Compassion is the ability to feel another's suffering and the desire to help relieve that suffering.   Self-compassion is compassion that is directed toward ourselves. Compassion is what allows us to connect with others and experience our common humanity. The following are exercises for cultivating compassion.

Compassion: Part 1

1. Sit down, close your eyes, and relax.

2. Allow yourself to become silent and observe the thoughts, feelings, emotions, and sensations that arise within. Allow all these phenomena to present themselves to your awareness.

3. Think of someone who you love or care about; it can be a person or a pet.

4. As you think of the subject of your meditation, allow yourself to reflect on the reasons why you feel the way you do about it.

5. Think about their lives. What hardships did they experience? What did they suffer?

6. Allow yourself to experience what their suffering may have been like for them. Allow yourself to experience how they may have felt due to the challenges they faced. Allow yourself to experience their pain as you understand it.

7. When you experience their pain, do so with complete acceptance. Do not try to deny it, change it, or cure it. Allow their pain to be a guest in your own heart. Allow your guest to fully express itself.

8. When you feel that you have experienced their suffering, allow yourself to feel love for the subject of your meditation.

Compassion: Part 2

1. Sit down, close your eyes, and relax.

2. Allow yourself to become silent and observe the thoughts, feelings, emotions, and sensations that arise within. Allow all these phenomena to present themselves to your awareness.

3. Now, think of someone for whom you have neutral feelings. It could be someone you do not personally know, or it could be someone you know but have no emotional involvement with.

4. Imagine what their life may be like. Imagine what hardships they may have experienced. Imagine their sufferings. It is okay if you do not know about their suffering; try to imagine the difficulties that they may have suffered.

5. Allow yourself to experience what their suffering may have been like. Allow yourself to experience how they may have felt due to the challenges they faced. Allow yourself to experience their pain as you understand it.

6. When you experience their pain, do so with complete acceptance. Do not try to deny it, change it, or cure it. Allow their pain to be a guest in your own heart. Allow your guest to fully express itself.

7. When you feel you have experienced their suffering, allow yourself to feel love for the subject of your meditation.

Compassion: Part 3

1. Sit down, close your eyes, and relax.

2. Allow yourself to become silent and observe the thoughts, feelings, emotions, and sensations that arise within. Allow all these phenomena to present themselves to your awareness.

3. Now, think of someone you know who has caused you frustration or anger.

4. Imagine what their life may be like. Imagine what hardships they may have

experienced. Imagine what they may have suffered. It is okay if you do not know about their suffering; try to imagine the difficulties that they have suffered.

5. Allow yourself to experience what their suffering may have been like. Allow yourself to experience how they may have felt due to the challenges they faced. Allow yourself to experience their pain as you understand it.

6. When you experience their pain, do so with complete acceptance. Do not try to deny it, change it, or cure it. Allow their pain to be a guest in your own heart. Allow your guest to fully express itself.

7. When you feel that you have experienced their suffering, allow yourself to feel love for the subject of your meditation.

Compassion: Part 4

1. Sit down, close your eyes, and relax.

2. Allow yourself to become silent and observe the thoughts, feelings, emotions, and sensations that arise within. Allow all these phenomena to present themselves to your awareness.

3. Now, think of yourself.

4. Reflect on how you have suffered in your life.

5. Allow yourself to think of the challenges that you have faced, the challenges that you are facing now, and the challenges you expect to face. Allow yourself to experience the pain or fear that comes with your suffering.

6. When you experience your suffering, do so with complete acceptance. Do not try to deny it, change it, or cure it. Allow your pain to be a guest in your own heart. Allow your guest to fully express itself.

7. When you feel that you have fully experienced your suffering, allow yourself to feel love for yourself.

Letting Go

Letting go of the past is never easy, and it can take a lot of work to get there. However, being able to let go of the past is essential if you are to bring healing to your inner child and take charge of your life.

The Meaning of "Letting Go"

"Letting go" can have a variety of meanings—some of which are very profound. However, for the purpose of this workbook, "letting go" refers to no longer holding on to a painful past.

To let go of the past does not mean to deny that it happened or to forget about it. Rather, letting go means that you no longer allow the past to dictate how you live today or in the future.

Letting go is about not allowing your thoughts and feelings to be consumed by the pains of your past. You acknowledge what happened in the past but place your focus on what is happening in the present moment rather than allowing your past to frame the present moment. When you focus on the present moment, you can direct your future.

Why Letting Go Is Necessary

One of the challenges of being human is that we have a deep need for certainty, yet life is anything but certain. How many times have you experienced a situation where your body is in one place, but your mind is somewhere else? You may be walking along a beautiful beach, but your mind is on your worries or concerns. If you are focused on your worries or concerns, you cannot be present. If you cannot be present, you cannot let go of the past.

The past no longer exists except in our minds, just as the future does not exist except in our minds. The only thing that exists is the present moment. Our wounded inner child can still trigger us to react because we are holding on to the past, though we may be holding on to it subconsciously.

If we acknowledge the past but focus on the present moment, we are letting go. By focusing on the present moment instead of our painful past, we can transform our lives. The reason for this is that life offers endless opportunities in every moment. When we are holding on to the past or our concerns for the future, those thoughts prevent us from becoming aware of those opportunities in the present moment. Instead, we develop limiting beliefs about ourselves and what we are capable of.

Letting Go and Mindfulness

Mindfulness is not just a spiritual or metaphysical practice that is engaged in by mystics or seekers; it is both a vital aspect of our happiness as well as being a precious gift that comes with being a conscious being. Without mindfulness, we cannot become fully actualized human beings; rather, we become reactive to situations and events. Instead of using our potential to expand our awareness, we live our lives based on a stimulus-response existence.

Most of our problems are directly linked to our inability to be fully present in our lives. Because we are not fully present, we lack clarity of awareness and wisdom when dealing with the challenges that we face, resorting instead to imposing solutions that are based on habit, fear, expediency, or rushed judgment.

To be fully actualized as a human is to be able to access the wisdom and awareness that are needed to create value, a value that benefits both us and others. This creation of value can only come from being fully aware of what is happening at any given moment, both within us and outside us. Without this awareness, we stumble through life and often create suffering for ourselves and those around us.

How to Let Go

One of the most powerful ways to let go of the past is to forgive it. The topic of forgiveness was already covered earlier in this chapter. However, as forgiveness is such an essential part of letting go, we will continue to discuss it here. The following are exercises and suggestions for using forgiveness to let go of the past:

Letting Go by Forgiving Others

There are two basic ways to forgive others. Which way you use them will depend on the nature of the relationship. The first way involves relationships that fit the following categories:

- The relationship is meaningful to you, and you want to maintain it.

- Both parties are aware that there have been hurt feelings.

- Both parties would like to move forward together.

This method works best for long-standing relationships where the hurt feelings are due to forgivable actions.

The second way to forgive others has to do with those situations where you do not believe reconciliation is possible or do not wish to reconcile with the other person. Despite this, you retain deep anger for what happened.

This anger you are holding may come from a situation that occurred many years ago. In such situations, it is important to let go of your anger so that you can move on with your life.

For this second way of forgiving, you can write a letter to the person who hurt you.

When writing the letter, it is not for the purpose of sending it but rather to allow you to express your anger and hurt so that you can release it. It is important to note that forgiveness takes time. Whatever technique you use, stick with the process of letting go but be patient with yourself.

Letting Go by Forgiving Yourself

It is not uncommon for people to have a harder time forgiving themselves than it is for them to forgive others. However, forgiveness always begins with you. You alone have the power to forgive. It deserves repeating that when we are talking about forgiveness, we are talking about making the decision that we will not continue to hold on to our hurt or anger.

If you have trouble forgiving yourself, imagine that someone you love or care for is going through the same situation that you are. How would you treat them? What would you tell them? Try to extend the same love and care to yourself that you would for the other person.

Letting Go of an Insurmountable Past

Many of us have faced challenges that seem insurmountable. Perhaps it is the loss of a loved one or being diagnosed with a life-threatening illness. No matter how hopeless a situation may be, remember that you are able to decide how you are going to respond to it. You can either give in to your situation, or you can decide to move forward with your life, regardless of whether you have any control over it.

By becoming mindful of the present moment, you can focus on what is happening now rather than what happened in the past or your concerns for the future. If you have experienced severe trauma, I encourage you to seek professional help from a licensed therapist to help you move forward in your life.

Letting Go of a Past Relationship

When people enter a relationship, they often have expectations for the relationship. The challenge is that both partners are constantly changing and evolving.

Additionally, no one is perfect, and it is inevitable that both partners will make mistakes. The key to maintaining a healthy relationship is for both partners to acknowledge these things.

When partners hold hurt feelings toward each other, it creates toxicity in the relationship. If the hurt feelings that one holds toward a partner are due to actions that are unforgivable, it would be better to end the relationship or see a licensed therapist. Holding on to past pains in a relationship can only result in the death of the relationship. Two people may stay together, but there will be no growth or vitality in the relationship.

For a relationship to be successful, both partners need to be focused on the present moment. Both partners need to let go of the past pain and focus on what they can do to nurture the relationship.

Letting Go of Timelines

Most of us have learned to believe in the concept of linear time. In other words, we experience time as being sequential, where a series of events lead up to something: that there is a beginning and an end. Because of this, we view our lives that way.

You can think of your life as a line; there is a starting point, which is when you are born, and an end point, which is death. Everything that happens between your birth and death is represented as a point on the line. Learning to speak, learning to walk, your first day at school, entering the job market, and purchasing your first home are just a few examples of the dots on the line.

Because of our socialization, many of us believe that we are supposed to follow a certain timeline. Sometimes we may not follow that timeline, or our plans do not work out. When this happens, we may feel that we are going backward or that we are stuck. We may feel that we have failed or done something wrong. The following are examples:

- A person who is married gets divorced, or their spouse passes away. As a result, they must scale down their living situation because of their finances.

- A person has a successful career when they lose their job due to a company layoff.

- An older adult who has worked all their lives decides that they want to go back to school.

Situations such as these can lead us to feel that we are going backward or that we may have done something wrong.

This kind of thinking reflects our belief system, not reality itself. Life does not follow a straight line. There is a natural ebb and flow in life. Life is about continuous change, where things go back and forth or up and down. Consider the change of seasons or the changing of the tides.

The societal belief that the events of our lives should follow a line of continuous progress is unrealistic. It would be healthier to learn to embrace change and trust that every new situation provides us with a chance for growth and to explore our deeper potential and new opportunities.

Instead of viewing your life as a straight line, consider viewing it as a crooked path where you never know what is around the next bend. Regardless of what we are experiencing, we are all experiencing life, and each one of us is following our own unique path that has brought us to the place where we are now.

From a conventional perspective, taking a few steps backward may cause us to feel like we have failed or that something is wrong with us. From the perspective of higher awareness, taking a few steps backward may actually be a major step in the right direction where you can live the life you truly want and become the best version of yourself.

Letting Go of Past Perceptions

How you see yourself and your life is determined by your perceptions. In turn, your perceptions are shaped by your beliefs and experiences. Life is constantly changing; it would seem logical that our perceptions change as well. Unfortunately, many of us live out our lives in our comfort zones. We remain there, where we restrict our lives by exposing ourselves only to the environments that we are familiar with. We interact with the people and experiences that we are comfortable with.

Because of this, our perceptions tend to remain largely the same. The danger of this is that our perceptions do not change with the changing times. Unless you broaden your experience, your perception of yourself and your world will remain unchanged. When your life remains unchanged, the issues you are faced with will remain unchanged as well. For these reasons, it is important to view yourself and your life in new ways. For that to happen, you need to let go of your past perceptions.

Letting Go of Past Beliefs

Our beliefs determine how we perceive the world, how we make decisions, and the actions we are willing to take. If you are holding on to past beliefs that do not empower you, it is imperative that you let go of them if you want to achieve the life that you desire. The challenge is that we often mistake our beliefs for reality.

Beliefs are just an interpretation that we make for ourselves. They are an interpretation of our experiences, both of our world and ourselves. Because of this, you have the power to change your beliefs by changing the way you interpret things.

At the most basic level, beliefs guide us toward positive outcomes and away from negative ones. If you are afraid of public speaking, it is because you have the belief that you are not good at it or that you may make a mistake, which would be embarrassing. In this case, your fear of public speaking is based on a belief. Your belief is keeping you from experiencing the negative outcome that you think may happen if you speak publicly.

Now imagine this. What would happen if someone told you that they would pay you $10,000 if you spoke publicly to a group? This kind of offer may get you to change the way you feel about public speaking. If you decide to speak publicly, it is because you have changed your beliefs. You are now focusing on the positive outcomes that you would enjoy if you agreed to the offer.

This example of public speaking illustrates how you can change your beliefs. You can let go of a current belief by reflecting on all the ways that this belief has cost you in your life. As you think about all the ways your beliefs have created negative outcomes for you, experience them emotionally. Feel the pain that you have endured for holding on to that belief.

Next, come up with a new belief that will empower you. When you do that, focus on all the ways that you would experience a positive outcome by adopting that belief. When you do this, get in touch with the positive emotions that you feel. If you repeat this process over a period of a few weeks, your new belief will become your way of thinking. The following is an example:

Let's say that you believe you cannot get ahead financially. No matter how hard you try, you struggle to make ends meet. This belief helps shape how you see yourself and the life you are living. Because of this belief, you have a scarcity mindset. You focus on the lack that exists in your world.

Earlier, I mentioned that our beliefs guide us away from negative outcomes and toward positive ones. If this is the case, then why would you have the belief that you cannot get ahead financially? While having this belief creates much negativity in your life, you do gain a benefit from it.

This benefit may be strong enough to keep you holding on to this belief. Perhaps when you were younger, you were taught that money is evil or that people who have a lot of money only think of themselves. If you start focusing on the negatives of holding on to this belief, you will realize that the negative outcomes outweigh the positive ones.

Let's say that you develop a new belief, such as "I can change my life if I am determined." If you think of all the ways that you would benefit by adopting this belief, then it will provide you with a new way of directing your attention and actions. This is why it is important to identify the beliefs that are limiting you and let go of them.

Exercises for Letting Go

The following exercises will help let go of the past for a variety of situations:

Exercise 2: Letting Go to Live in the Present Moment

In preparation for doing this exercise, I recommend that you set a timer for five minutes. With practice, you will no longer need the timer.

1. Get into a comfortable position and close your eyes.

2. Place your attention on your breath. Notice the bodily sensations that you experience as you breathe.

3. Continue to focus on your breathing and the accompanying sensations. Anytime that your mind wanders, return your attention to your breath without judging yourself or what you are experiencing. If it helps you, you can repeat a mantra while focusing on your breath.

4. When the five minutes are up, pay attention to how your body feels. Do you feel more relaxed?

5. Record your experiences in your journal.

6. Repeat this exercise daily for a week. If you do this, you will find this exercise becomes easier, and you will feel an even greater calm.

In the previous exercise, you practiced mindfulness by focusing on your breath without judging your experience. Happiness comes out of mindfulness because you are no longer judging. This next exercise also involves mindfulness. However, instead of focusing on your breath, you will focus on the world around you.

Exercise 3: Letting Go to Become Happy

This next exercise is best done after you have practiced Exercise 2 for a week. Exercise 2 was intended to strengthen your concentration, which is needed for this exercise. In Exercise 3, you will experience happiness by focusing on the present moment:

Take a 15-minute walk outside. As you walk, focus on the world around you without any judgment. Look at the sky, trees, cars, or whatever you experience.

If you find your mind wandering, return your attention to the world around you.

With practice, you will find yourself drawn to the things that make you happy.

Pay attention to how you feel when you remain in the present moment. Notice how a sense of happiness naturally fills you.

Exercise 4: Letting Go to Become Happy (an alternative exercise)

Exercise 4 is like Exercise 3, but it does not involve walking. It is important that you perform these exercises with an attitude of openness and non-judgment. Since the goal of mindfulness is to be aware of the present moment, do not allow your mind to deceive you with any positive or negative thoughts that you may experience while doing these exercises. Allow all thoughts to appear with full acceptance but keep your focus on the exercises.

1. Sit down and view your surroundings, taking your time to take everything in.

2. When you are ready, close your eyes and allow yourself to relax.

3. Imagine that you are an alien from a distant planet who has arrived on Earth to study it. You have no information about this planet, nor do you have any experience

to draw from. Because of this, you are unable to define, identify, analyze, or judge anything that you experience. In other words, you are a blank slate.

4. Now open your eyes and look at your surroundings again. Take your time.

5. How did your experience observing compare with your first observation?

If you did not notice any difference between the two observations, practice this exercise until you do.

Exercise 4: Letting Go of Anger

Anger is a natural emotion that we all experience from time to time. However, many of us do not handle our anger in a healthy way. We may express it in a way that we later regret, or we may keep it inside until we erupt.

Next time you feel anger, take a moment to challenge it. Take time to be with your anger and examine it. Take thirty minutes just to be with yourself. Ask yourself what you need to do to feel better about the situation. Perhaps you need to go for a walk or a run. Maybe it is doing something creative. Whatever you choose to do, place your focus on what you are doing. Also, pay attention to what you are experiencing in your body. Are you feeling more relaxed?

If your mind wanders, return it to the task that you are doing. Do so without any judgment.

When you are feeling more relaxed, you can determine if the reason for your anger is something that you can control or if it is something that you should just let go of.

If your anger is about something that you can control, then develop a plan of action. If it is something that is beyond your control, then keep your focus on being in the present moment.

Exercise 5: Letting Go for Self-Forgiveness

Think back to when you were a child and you made a mistake that emotionally impacted you. Now think of a small child and imagine that they made the same mistake. As your adult self, what would you tell the child? How would you comfort that child? What would you say to them? The child that you are comforting is you—your inner child.

Chapter Writing Prompts

Writing prompts can be a powerful way to access your subconscious mind and connect with your inner child. When writing, do not think about it too much. Instead, write down whatever comes to mind. Let your writing flow as thoughts appear. By doing this, you will gain insight into your inner child's pain.

Choose from the writing prompts below and respond to them in your journal.

1. Think of a specific situation where you had a hard time forgiving someone. What was the reason that made it difficult for you to forgive them? How do you feel about it today? Can you forgive them now?

2. Think about a time when you were forgiven. Who was the one who forgave you? How did you feel about the situation before you were forgiven? How can you use what you learned from the situation to forgive others?

3. What would need to happen before you could forgive yourself? Are those conditions realistic? Are you being compassionate to yourself?

4. Is there someone you believe you can never forgive? If so, what could you do to move on with your life and take care of your mental well-being?

5. Is there someone you need to forgive? Or is there something that you need to let

go of because it is holding you back? Write about it and why it is important for you to do so.

6. Do you have any unresolved traumas or emotions because you have not faced what you experienced? What is preventing you from facing it?

7. What is preventing you from letting go of past events that are holding you back?

8. Think back to a time when you felt stuck and could not get yourself to move forward with your life. What did you learn from that experience?

9. What emotions do you feel when you think about letting go of painful emotions from your past or your limiting beliefs? What is it that makes you feel that way?

10. Think of a time when you were able to let go of something that was holding you back. How did you manage to let go of it? How was that situation different from the situation that you are struggling with now?

11. How would your life be different today if you were able to let go of your painful past?

12. What patterns of thinking or feeling keep you from being able to let go of your past? What could you do to change those thoughts or feelings?

13. Think about the regrets that you have. What could you do to reframe them so that they would serve you by providing you with important lessons?

14. Identify a situation from your past that still triggers a negative emotional response today. How could you change the way that you view the situation by approaching it with understanding and compassion?

15. What do you need to let go of so that you can live as your authentic self and live the life that you deserve?

16. What do you tell yourself that prevents you from letting go of your anger or resentment from the past?

17. Think about an experience that you still hold on to that causes you to react emotionally in a negative way. If there was something for which you could be grateful for having that experience, what would it be and why?

18. How do you hold yourself back from experiencing happiness or joy? What is causing you to do that? How does doing this help you today? Is it still worth doing it?

Conclusion

By completing the exercises in this workbook, you have taken a major step in expanding your awareness of your inner child. However, this is still just the beginning. It is important that you apply what you learned from this workbook in your daily life. Also, revisit the exercises in this book as often as you feel necessary. By doing this, you will reinforce what you have learned.

The important thing is to understand that healing your inner child takes daily work. It is the culmination of all your efforts that will eventually transform the way that you feel about yourself.

References

Carson, J. W., Keefe, F. J., Lynch, T. R., Carson, K. M., Goli, V., Fras, A. M., & Thorp, S. R. (2005). Loving-kindness meditation for chronic low back pain: Results from a pilot trial. *Journal of Holistic Nursing* *23*(3), 287–304. https://doi.org/10.1177/0898010105277651

Desai, R. (2020). Stress has made us shallow breathers. Here's what it does to our bodies. *The Swaddle.* https://theswaddle.com/stress-has-made-us-shallow-breathers-heres-what-it-does-to-our-bodies/

Flook, L., Goldberg, S. B., Pinger, L., Bonus, K., & Davidson, R. J. (2013). Mindfulness for teachers: A pilot study to assess effects on stress, burnout, and teaching efficacy. *Mind, Brain and Education, 7*(4), p. 256. https://doi.org/10.1111/mbe.12026

Hoge, E. A., Chen, M. M., Orr, E., Metcalf, C. A., Fischer, L. E., Pollack, M. H., De Vivo, I., & Simon, N. M. (2013). Loving-Kindness meditation practice associated with longer telomeres in women. *Brain, Behavior, and Immunity, 32,* 159–163. https://doi.org/10.1016/j.bbi.2013.04.005

Orentas, G. (2021). Signs and symptoms of PTSD in women. Psych Central.

Zeidan, F., & Vago, D. R. (2016). Mindfulness meditation-based pain relief: A mechanistic account. *Annals of the New York Academy of Sciences, 1373*(1), 114–127. https://doi.org/10.1111/nyas.13153

12665085R00063

PROBLEM SOLVING™

WITH MATH MODELS

FOURTH GRADE

DR. NICKI NEWTON

Giggle Nook Publications
Math with a Smile

Gigglenook Publication

P.O. Box 110134

Trumbull CT 06611

Email: gigglenook@gmail.com

Website: www.drnicki123.com

Produced by GiggleNook Publications

Thank you to the entire Production staff

Chief Operating Officer: Dr. Nicki Newton

Publisher: Gigglenook Publication

Cover Design: This Way Up Productions

Printed in the United States of America through CreateSpace, LLC

ISBN-13: 978-1492194392

ISBN-10: 1492194395

Volume 1: December 2012

Dedicated to Mom and Pops, Always

PROBLEM SOLVING™
WITH MATH MODELS
FOURTH GRADE

DR. NICKI NEWTON

TABLE OF CONTENTS

FOREWORD

Story problems can be great! Story problems are the stuff life is made of. If we can make connections for children between their daily lives and the problems we pose and solve in school, we will have much more success. We need to provide scaffolds into the process.

The New Math Common Core (2010) places a big emphasis on problem solving. The first mathematical practice mentioned states that students should "Make sense of problems and persevere in solving them." It goes on to describe this by stating that mathematically proficient students should be able to explain a problem and find ways to enter into it. According to the New Math Common Core students should be able to solve problems with objects, drawings and equations. In this book, students will practice word problems aligned to the standards by using the CCSS designated math models.

The Math Common Core, actually adopted the framework for story problems, created by Carpenter, Fennema, Franke, Levi & Empson, 1999; Peterson, Fennema & Carpenter (1989). The research says that the more teachers understand these types of problems and teach them to their students, the better students understand the problems and are able to solve them. Furthermore, the research makes the case that the KEY WORD METHOD should be avoided! Students should learn to understand the problem types and what they are actually discussing rather than "key word" tricks. The thing about key words is that they only work with really simplistic problems and so as students do more sophisticated work with word problems, the key words do not serve them well. They may actually lead them in the wrong direction, often encouraging the wrong operation. For example, given this problem: *John has 2 apples. Kate has 3 more than he does. How many do they have altogether?* Many students just add 2 and 3 instead of unpacking the problem. Another example, given this problem: *Sue has 10 marbles. She has 2 times as many marbles as Lucy. How many marbles does Lucy have?*

Problem Solving with Math Models© 2012

Often times, students just multiply because they see the word times, instead of really reading and understanding the problem.

This book is about giving students a repertoire of tools, models and strategies to help them think about, understand and solve word problems. We want to scaffold reasoning opportunities from the concrete (using objects) to the pictorial (pictures and drawings) and, finally, to the abstract (writing equations).

DR. NICKI NEWTON

ACKNOWLEDGEMENTS

I would like to thank many people for their support, expertise, guidance, and encouragement during this project. First of all I would like to thank God, without him this would not be possible. Second, I would like to thank my mom, pa, big mom, and granddaddy. Third, I would like to thank my family for all their love and support, especially my Tia that calls me every day and asks me "What have you accomplished today?" And I would like to thank all of my friends that support me all the time. Finally, I would like to thank the many people who were part of the Gigglenook Book Production Team. This book series would not have been possible without the continual support of all of them.

INTRODUCTION TO THE TYPES OF WORD PROBLEMS

Grade Specific Problem Solving Expectations

The CCSSM (2010) is very specific about what students should be able to do in terms of solving word problems by grade level. There are 4 general categories for addition and subtraction problems. In kindergarten students are exposed to 4 problem types - 1 addition, 1 subtraction, and 2 part/part whole problems. They are expected to work with these types of problems through 10. But, in first grade, there is a big leap. The standards say that the children will be able to work with the above-mentioned four problems, in addition to addition and subtraction change unknown problems, the other part/ part whole problem as well as comparison problems with unknowns in all positions and with a symbol for the unknown to represent the problem through 20. They should also be able to solve word problems with three numbers adding up to 20. By second grade, they have to do the same thing with all problem types, including the harder comparison problems through 100. In 3rd through 5th grade the students should be able to solve all of the problem types using larger whole numbers, fractions and decimals.

Adding to Problems

"Adding to" problems are all about adding. There are three types. The first type is *Adding to* problems where the result is unknown. For example, *Jenny had 5 marbles. John gave her 3 more. How many marbles does Jenny have now?* In this problem the result is unknown. Teachers tend to tell these types of problems. They are basic and straightforward. The teacher should start with concrete items, then proceed to drawing out the story, then to diagramming the story, and finally to using equations to represent the story. This is the easiest type of story problem to solve.

The second kind of *Adding to* problem is the "Change Unknown" problem. For example, *Jenny had 5 marbles. John gave her some more. Now she has 8 marbles. How many marbles did John give her?* In this type of problem, the students are looking for the change. They know the start and they know the end but they don't know the *change*. So, students have to put down the start and then count up to find how many. Students could also start with 8 marbles and take away the original 5 to see how many more were added to make 8.

The third type of *Adding to* Problem is a "Start Unknown" problem. For example, *Jenny had some marbles. John gave her 3 more. Now she has 8 marbles. How many marbles did Jenny have in the beginning?* In this type of problem, the students are looking for the start. This is the hardest type of *adding to* problem to solve. This takes a great deal of modeling.

Taking From Problems

Taking From problems are all about subtracting. There are three types. The first type is *taking from* problems where the result is unknown. For example, *Jenny had 5 marbles. She gave John 3. How many marbles does Jenny have left?* In this problem, the result is unknown. Teachers tend to tell these types of problems. They are basic and straightforward. The teacher should start with concrete items, then proceed to drawing out the story, then to diagramming the story, and finally to writing equations to represent the story.

The second kind of *Taking From* problem is the "Change Unknown" problem. For example, *Jenny had 10 marbles. She gave John some. Now she has 8 marbles left. How many marbles did she give to John?* In this type of problem, the students are looking for the change. They know the start and they know the end but they don't know the *change*. So, students have to put down the start and then count up to find how many. Students could also start with 10 marbles and take away some until they have 8 left. They would count to see how many they had to take away to remain with 8.

The third type of *Taking From* problem is a "Start Unknown" problem. For example, *Jenny had some marbles. She gave John 3. Now she has 7 marbles left. How many marbles did Jenny have to start with?* In this type of problem, the students are looking for the start. This is the hardest type of *taking from* problem to solve. This takes a great deal of modeling. You can use ten frames to show this. One strategy is to have the students put down the seven she has left and count up three to see how many that makes.

Part/Part Whole Problems

A *Part/Part Whole* problem is a problem that discusses the two parts and the whole. There are three types of *Part/Part Whole* Problems. The first is a problem where the *whole* is unknown. For example, *Susie has some marbles. Five are red and five are blue. How many marbles does she have altogether?* We know both parts and the task is to figure out the whole.

The second kind of problem is a problem where one of the *parts* is unknown. For example, *Susie has 10 marbles. Seven are red. The rest are blue. How many are blue?* In this type of problem, we are given the whole and one of the parts. The task is to figure out the other part.

The third type of problem is a *Both Addends Unknown* problem. In this type of problem both addends are not known, only the total is given. For example, *There are 4 frogs on the log. Some are blue and some are green. There are some of each color. How many of each color could there be?* The task is to figure out all the possible combinations.

Comparing Stories

Comparing Stories are the most difficult types of stories to tell. There are three types of comparison stories. The first type of comparing story is where two different things are being compared. For example, *Susie has ten lollipops and Kayla had eight. How many more lollipops did Susie have than Kayla?*

The second type of comparing story is where the bigger part is unknown. In this type of story, we are looking for the bigger amount. For example, *Susie had 4 candies. Maya had 3 more than her. How many candies did Maya have?* Here, we know what Susie had, and then in comparison, Maya had 3 more. The task is to find the bigger part.

The third type of comparing story is to find the smaller part. This is the hardest type of story to tell. For example, *Jaya has 7 candies. She has 3 more than Marcos. How many does Marcos have? In this type of story we know what Jaya has and we know that she has 3 more than Marcos.* We are looking for the smaller amount. We only know about what Marcos has in comparison to what Jaya has. The task is to use the information given to solve for the smaller part.

Two Step Problems

Starting in second grade, students start to do two-step problems where they combine the problem types. For example: *Sue had 5 more marbles than David. David had 4 marbles. How many marbles do they have altogether?* To solve two-step problems, students should have a good understanding of the original problem types and then these are combined into a more complex problem.

THE 4ᵀᴴ GRADE WORD PROBLEM STANDARDS (CCSSM, 2010)

4OA3: Solve multistep word problems posed with whole numbers. Represent these problems using equations with a letter standing for the unknown quantity.

4NF3: Solve word problems involving addition and subtraction, e.g., by using visual fraction models and equations to represent the problem.

4NF7: Compare two decimals to hundredths...Record the results of comparisons with the symbols >, =, or <, and justify the conclusions, e.g., by using a visual model.

4MD1: Know relative sizes of measurement units within one system of units including km, m, cm; kg, g; lb., oz.; l, ml; hr, min, sec. Record measurement equivalents in a two-column table.

4MD2: Use the four operations to solve word problems involving distances, intervals of time, liquid volumes, masses of objects, and money, including problems involving simple fractions or decimals, and problems that require expressing measurements given in a larger unit in terms of a smaller unit.

4MD3: Apply the area and perimeter formulas for rectangles in real world and mathematical problems.

4MD4: Make a line plot to display a data set of measurements in fractions of a unit (1/2, 1/4, 1/8). Solve problems involving addition and subtraction of fractions by using information presented in line plots.

4MD7: Solve addition and subtraction problems to find unknown angles on a diagram in real world and mathematical problems, e.g., by using an equation with a symbol for the unknown angle measure.

INTRODUCING THE MODELS FOR THINKING

There are several great tools to use for solving number stories. In this book students will use a few different tools to think about the word problems. The CCSSM (2010) Standards state that students should use "objects, drawings, diagrams and acting out" to solve problems. In 4ᵗʰ grade students should be able to:

USE EQUATIONS

4OA3: Represent problems using equations with a letter standing for the unknown quantity.

$$4 + x = 29$$

$$345 - x = 49$$

4MD7: Recognize angle measure as additive. Use an equation with a symbol for the unknown angle measure to solve problems.

$$56° + 34° + x = 180°$$

USE DRAWINGS

4NF3: Use visual fraction models and equations to represent the problem.

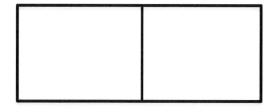

4NF7: Compare decimals with the symbols >, =, or <, and justify the conclusions, e.g., by using a visual model.

$$.40 > .25 \qquad .8 < .9 \qquad .50 + .20 = .70$$

USE TABLES

4MD1: Record measurement equivalents in a two-column table.

Centimeters	Meters
100	1
200	2
300	3
400	4
500	5

USE OPEN NUMBERLINES

4MD2: Represent measurement quantities using diagrams such as number line diagrams that feature a measurement scale.

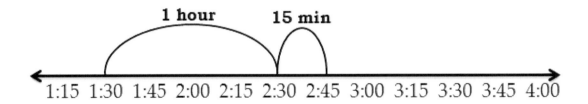

Students also use the open number line for other types of problems. They draw a line, plot numbers on it and count using a variety of strategies. For example, let's take the problem 45 plus 37.

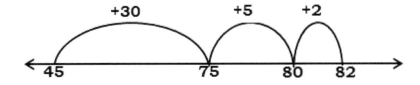

The student starts at 45 and jumps 30 because they broke apart the 37 into 30, plus 5, plus 2. From 75, they jump five more to 80 and then 2 more to 82. Number lines are a huge part of the new math CCSS and it is very important to make sure that students are very

Problem Solving with Math Models© 2012

comfortable using them. Students will use number lines throughout the different grades.

USE DOUBLE OPEN NUMBER LINE

The double number line is a great model for comparing two different things. For example, *Sue had 15 apples and Josie had 4 more than she did. How many did Josie have?*

Students draw a line and then plot one part of the comparison on the top and the other part of the comparison on the bottom. (See below)

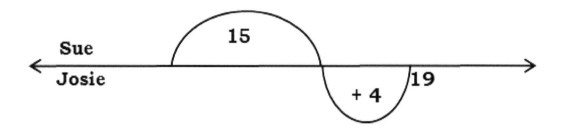

USE FORMULAS

4MD3: Apply the area and perimeter formulas for rectangles in real world and mathematical problems.

$$\text{Perimeter} = 2(\text{length} + \text{width})$$

$$\text{Area} = L \times W$$

CREATE LINE PLOTS

4MD4: Make a line plot to display a data set of measurements in fractions of a unit (1/2, 1/4, 1/8). Solve problems involving addition and subtraction of fractions by using information presented in line plots.

The 4th grade made a frequency table of sizes of plants. Use the data in the frequency table to make a line plot.

4½, 5, 5, 5, 5, 6, 7, 7, 7, 7, 7, 7½, 7½, 7½

Line plot of pets per person in our classroom

```
                                        X
                          X             X
                          X             X     X
                          X             X     X
                    X     X     X       X     X
  ←─────────────────────────────────────────────────→
      1     2     3     4     4½    5     6     7    7½
```

Line plot questions:

1. What was the length of the longest flower?
2. What was the length of the shortest flower?
3. What is the difference between the lengths of the shortest and longest flowers?

Problem Solving with Math Models© 2012

USE BAR/TAPE DIAGRAM

In the CCSSM students are required to know how to use a tape diagram to model their thinking. *Bar diagrams help students to "unpack" the structure of a problem and lay the foundation for its solution"* (Diezmann and English, 2001, p. 77 cited in Charles, Monograph 24324). *Nickerson (1994) found that the ability to use diagrams is integral to mathematics thinking and learning (cited in Charles).*

In the charts below, I have provided a detailed explanation for each of the CCSS 1-step word problem types for addition and subtraction. The word problem type is designated with a sample problem. Then there is a bar diagram to show the relationships between the quantities. Then there is an explanation of the problem type and the various strategies that can be used to solve the problem. There is also the algebraic equation showing the different operations that can be used to solve the problem. As Charles (Monograph 24324) points out, *"It is important to recognize that a relationship in some word problems can be translated into more than one appropriate number sentence."*

Problem Types	Result Unknown	Change Unknown	Start Unknown
Join/Adding to	Marco had 5 marbles. His brother gave him 5 more. How many does he have now?	Marco had 5 marbles. His brother gave him some more. Now he has 10. How many did his brother give him?	Marco had some marbles. His brother gave him 5 more. Now he has 10. How many did he have in the beginning?
Bar Diagram Modeling Problem	? ←——————→ | 5 | 5 |	10 ←——————→ | 5 | ? |	10 ←——————→ | ? | 5 |
What are we looking for? Where is X?	Both addends are known. We are looking for the total amount. The result is the unknown. In other words, we know what we started with and we know the change, we are looking for the end.	The first addend is known. The result is also known. We are looking for the change. The change is unknown. In other words, we know what happened at the start and we know what happened at the end. We are looking for the change. We need to find out what happened in the middle.	The second addend is known. The result is known. We are looking for the start. The start is unknown. In other words, we know the change and we know the end but we don't know what happened at the beginning.
Algebraic Sentence	5 + 5 = ?	5 + ?= 10 10-5=?	x + 5 = 10
Strategies to Solve	Add/ Know number Bonds/Know derived Facts/ Count Up	Count Up/Know Bonds/	Count up/Subtract
Answer	5 + 5 = 10 He had ten marbles.	5 + 5 = 10 10 - 5 = 5 He brother gave him five marbles.	5 + 5 = 10 10 - 5 = 5 He had five marbles.

Problem Solving with Math Models© 2012

Problem Types	Result Unknown	Change Unknown	Start Unknown
Separate/ Taking From	Marco had 10 marbles. He gave his brother 4. How many does he have left?	Marco had 10 marbles. He gave some away. Now he has 5 left. How many did he give away?	Marco had some marbles. He gave 2 away and now he has 5 left. How many did he have to start with?
Bar Diagram Modeling Problem			
What are we looking for? Where is X?	In this story we know the beginning and what happened in the middle. The mystery is what happened at the end. The result is unknown.	In this story we know the beginning and the end. The mystery is what happened in the middle. The change is unknown.	In this story we know what happened in the middle and what happened at the end. The mystery is how did it start. The start is unknown.
Algebraic Sentence	$10 - 4 = ?$	$10 - ? = 5$ $5 + x = 10$	$? - 2 = 5$ $2 + 5 = ?$
Strategies to Solve	Subtract/ /Use number Bonds Facts/ Know derived Facts (Doubles -1, Doubles -2)	Subtract until you have the result left/ Count Up/Use number Bonds/Use derived facts	Count up/Subtract
Answer	$10 - 4 = 6$ He had 6 marbles left.	$10 - 5 = 5$ $5 + 5 = 10$ He gave away 5 marbles.	$7 - 2 = 5$ $2 + 5 = 7$ He had 7 marbles in the beginning.

Problem Types	Quantity Unknown	Part Unknown	Both Addends Unknown
Part/Part Whole/Putting together/Taking Apart	Marco has 5 red marbles and 5 blue ones. How many marbles does Marco have? $5 + 5 = x$	Marco has 10 marbles. Five are red and the rest are blue. How many are blue? $10 - 5 =$ or $5 + x = 10$	Marco has 10 marbles. Some are red and some are blue. How many could be red and how many could be blue?
Bar Diagram Modeling Problem	? \[5 | 5 \]	10 \[5 | ? \]	10 \[? | ? \]
What are we looking for? Where is X?	In this type of story we are talking about a group, set or collection of something. Here we know both parts and we are looking for the total.	In this type of story we are talking about a group, set or collection of something. Here we know the total and one of the parts. We are looking for the amount of the other part.	In this type of story we are talking about a group, set or collection of something. Here we know the total but we are to think about all the possible ways to make the group, set or collection.
Algebraic Sentence	$5 + 5 = ?$	$5 + ? = 10$ $10 - 5 = ?$	$x + y = 10$
Strategies to Solve	Add/ Know number Bonds/Know derived Facts/ Count Up	Count Up/Know Bonds/	Count up/Subtract
Answer	5+5=10 He had ten marbles.	5+5=10 10-5 =? Five were blue	1+9 4+6 9+1 6+4 2+8 5+5 8 + 2 3+7 10+0 0 +10 7+3 These are the possibilities

Problem Solving with Math Models© 2012

Problem Types	Difference Unknown	Bigger Part Unknown	Smaller Part Unknown
Compare	Marco has 5 marbles. His brother has 7. How many more marbles does his brother have than he does?	Marco has 5 marbles. His brother has 2 more than he does. How many marbles does his brother have?	Tom has 5 rocks. Marco has 2 less than Tom. How many rocks does Marco have?
Bar Diagram Modeling Problem	5 ? ↔ 7	5 5 2 ?	5 ?
What are we looking for? Where is X?	In this type of story we are comparing two amounts. We are looking for the difference between the two numbers.	In this type of story we are comparing two amounts. We are looking for the bigger part which is unknown.	In this type of story we are comparing two amounts. We are looking for the smaller part which is unknown.
Algebraic Sentence	7-5 =?	5 + ? = 7	5-2=?
Strategies to Solve	Count up/ Count back	Count up	Subtract
Answer	His brother had 2 more marbles than he did.	His brother had 7 marbles.	Marco had 3 marbles.

Teacher Tips:

- When you introduce the problem, be sure to tell the students what type of problem it is.

- Remember that you can take the same problem and rework it in different ways throughout the week.

- Work on a problem type until the students are proficient at recognizing and solving that problem type. Also give them opportunities to write and tell that specific problem type.

- Be sure to contextualize the problems in the students' everyday lives. Using the problems in the book as models, substitute the students' names and their everyday things.

- Be sure to provide tons of guided practice. Solve problems together as a class, with partners and in groups. Individual practice should come after the students have had plenty of opportunities to work together and comprehend and understand what they are doing.

- Emphasize that there is no one correct way to solve a problem but that there is usually only one correct answer.

- Encourage students to always show their work

CHAPTER 1
ADD TO RESULT UNKNOWN PROBLEMS

These types of problems are the easiest types of addition problems. In these problems students are looking for what happened at the end of the story. We know what we started with and what we added to that part. We are trying to find out how many we have altogether now.

PROBLEM	John had 10 marbles. Henry gave him 7 more. How many does he have now?
MODEL	
EQUATION	10 + 7 = ?

ADD TO RESULT UNKNOWN

1. Song A had 17,999 downloads on Monday. On Tuesday, it had 34,845 more downloads. How many downloads did it have altogether?

Way#1: Use friendly numbers to add. Which place could you round to get a friendly number in order to add quickly?

Way#2: Write an equation with a letter standing for the unknown.

Explain your thinking:

Problem Solving with Math Models© 2012

ADD TO RESULT UNKNOWN

2. Brett left his house at 7:05 a.m. He spent 45 minutes at Kurt's house and 25 minutes at Tom's house. How long was Brett gone?

Solve with an open number line

Explain your thinking:

ADD TO RESULT UNKNOWN

3. Lauren, the baker, used 557 grams of sugar in the cake mixture. Then she used 528 grams of sugar for the frosting. How many grams of sugar did she use for the cake altogether? Did she use more than a kilogram of sugar to make the cake?

Model with a tape diagram

Explain your thinking:

Problem Solving with Math Models© 2012

ADD TO RESULT UNKNOWN

4. Andy made fruit punch. First, he added 134 ml of cranberry juice, then he added 358 ml of pineapple juice, finally, he added 442 ml of banana juice. How many ml of juice did Andy put into the fruit punch altogether? Did he use more than a liter?

Model with a tape diagram

Explain your thinking:

ADD TO RESULT UNKNOWN

5. Jake had $99.10. He got $55.20 for his birthday. How much money does he have now?

Way#1: Solve with an equation

Way#2: Check in a different way

Explain your thinking:

ADD TO RESULT UNKNOWN

6. Miguel ran 2/3 of a mile in the morning and 1/3 of a mile in the afternoon. Did Miguel run over a mile?

Way#1: Solve with a number line

Way#2: Solve with a drawing

Explain your thinking:

ADD TO RESULT UNKNOWN

7. Farmer Kate built a yard for her chickens to run around in. It was 7 ft. long and 7 ft. wide. She found it to be too short. So she added 9 more feet to the length. What was the length of the fence with the addition? What was the perimeter of the fence with the addition? What is the area of the fence with the addition?

Draw an illustration to solve

Explain your thinking:

Problem Solving with Math Models© 2012

ADD TO RESULT UNKNOWN

8. Brittany made necklaces. She had 3ft. of string. She could make 1 necklace with 12 inches of string. How many necklaces can she make with 3 ft. of string?

Create a table to show your thinking

Necklace	Inches	Feet
1	12	1

Explain your thinking:

CHAPTER 1 QUIZ: ADD TO RESULT UNKNOWN

Solve with a model:

1. Fran made some fruit punch. She put in a quart of orange juice. Then she added a quart of apple juice. Finally, she added a quart of pineapple juice. How much fruit punch did she make? Did she make a gallon of punch? Show your work.

2. Clay made a dog run in his backyard. At first, he made a run that was 5ft. long and 5ft. wide. Then he decided to make it bigger. He added 2ft. to the length and 3ft. to the width. What is the perimeter of the new dog run? What is the area of the new dog run?

3. Maria ran 555 meters in the morning and 488 meters in the afternoon. How many meters did she run altogether? Did she run more than a kilometer?

4. Kelly had 3/6 of a yard of blue string. She bought 2/6 of a yard of yellow string and 4/6 of a yard of orange string. How much string does she have now? Does she have more than a yard?

CHAPTER 2
ADD TO CHANGE UNKNOWN PROBLEMS

In these problems students are looking for what happened in the middle of the story. In this type of story we know what happened at the beginning but then some change happened and now we have more than we started with at the end. We are trying to find out how many things were added in the middle of the story.

PROBLEM	John had 5 marbles. His mother gave him some more. Now he has 12. How many did his mother give him?
MODEL	+7 over arc from 5 to 12 on number line
EQUATION	5 + ? = 12

ADD TO CHANGE UNKNOWN

1. The candy store had 435 grams of chocolate fudge. They made some more fudge and now they have 1000 grams. How many grams of chocolate did they make?

Way#1: Solve with a number line

Way#2: Solve with an equation, use a letter for the unknown

Explain your thinking:

ADD TO CHANGE UNKNOWN

2. Javier went to the basketball court at 2:15 p.m. He went home at 4:07 p.m. How long was he at the basketball court?

Solve with a number line diagram

Explain your thinking:

Problem Solving with Math Models© 2012

ADD TO CHANGE UNKNOWN

3. Mr. Leroy walked 3/6 of a mile in the morning. In the afternoon he walked some more. By the end of the day he had walked 1 mile. How much did he walk in the afternoon?

Way#1: Solve with a number line

Way#2: Solve with an illustration

Explain your thinking:

ADD TO CHANGE UNKNOWN

4. Dina made fruit punch for the party. She added 400 ml of cherry juice and then some apple juice. Altogether, she had 1 liter of juice. How much apple juice did she use?

Way#1: Draw a picture of a beaker to solve

Way#2: Solve with an equation, use a letter for the unknown

Explain your thinking:

ADD TO CHANGE UNKNOWN

5. Sharon had $33.54. She got some more money for her birthday. Now she has $50.59. How much money did she get for her birthday?

Way#1: Solve with an equation, use a letter for the unknown

Way#2: Solve another way

Explain your thinking:

ADD TO CHANGE UNKNOWN

6. In a jumping competition, Kara jumped 55 centimeters for her first jump and then some more centimeters for her second jump. Altogether, she jumped 100 centimeters. How much did she jump for her second jump?

Way#1: Solve with an open number line

Way#2: Solve with an equation, use a letter for the unknown

Explain your thinking:

ADD TO CHANGE UNKNOWN

7. Farmer Sue built a fence for her rabbits. First she made a fence that was 7ft long and 7 ft. wide. Then she added some length to the fence. Now the length is 10 ft. long. How many feet did she add to the length of the fence altogether? What is the new perimeter of the yard?

Way#1: Solve with drawing

Way#2: Solve with an equation, use a letter for the unknown

Explain your thinking:

ADD TO CHANGE UNKNOWN

8. The bakery only had 3 ounces of fudge left in the morning. It made some more and now it has a pound. How many ounces of fudge did the bakery make?

Way#1: Model with a tape diagram

Way#2: Solve with an equation, use a letter for the unknown

Explain your thinking:

CHAPTER 2 QUIZ:
ADD TO CHANGE UNKNOWN PROBLEMS

Solve with a model:

1. Lois left her house at 2:07 p.m. She went to the store and then to her friend's house. She came back at 4:35 p.m. How long was she gone?

2. The pizza shack had 18 kilos of shredded cheese. They got some more and now they have 40 kilos. How much shredded cheese did they get?

3. Troy ran 2/5 of a mile in the morning. In the afternoon, he ran some more. By the evening, he had run 4/5 of a mile. How far did he run in the afternoon?

4. Kelly had $55.67. She got some more money and now she has $82.69. How much money did she get?

CHAPTER 3
ADD TO START UNKNOWN PROBLEMS

In these problems students are looking for what happened in the beginning of the story. In this type of story we know what happened in the middle and we know how many we ended up with but we are looking for how the story started.

PROBLEM	John had some marbles. Henry gave him 7 more. Now he has 14. How many did he have in the beginning?
MODEL	
EQUATION	$? + 7 = 14$

ADD TO START UNKNOWN

1. Song A had several downloads from the internet in the morning. In the afternoon, Song A got 25,456 more downloads. Now it has 35,987 downloads all total. How many downloads did it have in the morning?

Way#1: Solve with numbers

Way#2: Check in a different way

Explain your thinking:

Problem Solving with Math Models© 2012

ADD TO START UNKNOWN

2. Erica went to the mall for 3 and a half hours. She then went to her friend's house for 1 hour and 15 minutes. She came back to her house at 4:15 p.m. What time did she leave her house originally?

Solve with a number line diagram

Explain your thinking:

ADD TO START UNKNOWN

3. Clarise ran in the morning. Then she ran ¼ mile more. All total she ran ½ of a mile. How far did she run in the morning.

Way#1: Solve with a drawing

Way#2: Solve with an equation, use a letter for the unknown

Explain your thinking:

ADD TO START UNKNOWN

4. Timothy had some money. For his birthday he got $45.44. Now he has $57.55. How much did he have in the beginning?

Way#1: Solve with an equation, use a letter for the unknown

Way#2: Check in a different way

Explain your thinking:

ADD TO START UNKNOWN

5. The school cook made some liters of fruit punch. He then made 15 more liters. Altogether he made 70 liters of fruit punch. How much fruit punch did he have in the beginning?

Way#1: Model with a drawing

Way#2: Solve with an equation, use a letter for the unknown

Explain your thinking:

Problem Solving with Math Models© 2012

ADD TO START UNKNOWN

6. Jay had some marbles. Tim gave him 23 more. His sister gave him 35 more. Now he has 70 marbles. How many marbles did he have to start with?

Way#1: Model with a tape diagram

Way#2: Solve with an equation, use a letter for the unknown

Explain your thinking:

ADD TO START UNKNOWN

7. The baker made some pies. He cut up several apples. Then he ran out of apples and needed some more. So, he cut up 3 ½ more cups of apples. In total, he cut up 5 cups of apples. How many cups did he cut up in the beginning?

Way#1: Solve with an illustration

Way#2: Solve with an equation, use a letter for the unknown

Explain your thinking:

Problem Solving with Math Models© 2012

ADD TO START UNKNOWN

8. Jonathan ran a bit in the morning. Then he ran 4/7 of a mile more. Altogether, he ran 6/7 of a mile. How much did he run in the morning?

Way#1: Solve with a number line

Way#2: Solve with an equation, use a letter for the unknown

Explain your thinking:

CHAPTER 3 QUIZ:
ADD TO START UNKNOWN PROBLEMS

Solve with a model:

1. Kelly had some string to make bracelets. She bought 89 more centimeters of string. Now she has 207 centimeters of string. How much string did she have in the beginning? How many meters of string does she have now?

2. Chung went to his grandmothers for 2 1/2 hours. Then he went to his cousin's house for another hour. He came home at 5:25. What time did he leave his house?

3. Chef Hong made a fancy soup. He put in some coconut juice and then he added 556 more ml of coconut juice. Altogether, he used 1023 ml of coconut juice. How much coconut juice did he have in the fancy soup in the beginning? Did he put in more than a liter altogether?

4. Steven ran on Monday morning. On Tuesday, he ran 2 more kilometers. On Wednesday, he ran another 3 kilometers. Altogether, he ran 8 kilometers. How many kilometers did he run on Monday morning?

UNIT 1 TEST:
ADDITION PROBLEMS

Solve with a model:

1. The jewelry store had 100 rings. They got a shipment of 15 more on Monday, 59 more on Tuesday, and 46 more on Wednesday. How many rings do they have now?

2. Raul ran 1/6 of a mile in the morning, 2/6 of a mile in the afternoon and 3/6 of a mile in the evening. How far did Raul run? Did he run at least a mile?

Problem Solving with Math Models© 2012

3. Farmer Jen made a cage for her turtles. It was 4 feet long and 7 feet wide. What was the perimeter of the cage? What was the area of the cage?

4. Ichiro, the baker, made some fudge. He made some fudge to start with and then he made 849 more grams of it. He made 1 kilo of fudge altogether. How much did he make in the beginning?

CHAPTER 1
TAKE FROM RESULT UNKNOWN PROBLEMS

In these problems students are looking for what happened in the end of the story. In this type of story we know what happened at the beginning and also what change occurred. We are trying to find out how many things remained after some things were taken away.

PROBLEM	John had 10 apples. He gave 5 away. How many does he have left?
MODEL	
EQUATION	10 – ? = 5

TAKE FROM RESULT UNKNOWN

1. Daniel had $352. He paid $55 for some shoes, $38 for some videos, and $207 for some clothes. How much money did he have left?

Way#1: Solve with an open number line

Way#2: Solve with an equation, use a letter for the unknown

Explain your thinking:

TAKE FROM RESULT UNKNOWN

2. Baker Maria had 2 kilograms of cookies. She sold 234 grams in the morning, 612 grams in the afternoon and 908 grams in the evening. How many grams does she have left? Did she sell more than a kilogram of cookies?

Way#1: Model with a tape diagram

Way#2: Solve with an equation, use a letter for the unknown

Explain your thinking:

TAKE FROM RESULT UNKNOWN

3. Sara had 5 meters of wood. She needed 100 centimeters for each shelf that she was making. How many shelves could she make?

Way#1: Model with a table

Shelves	Centimeters	Meters
1	100	1

Way#2: Solve with an equation, use a letter for the unknown

Explain your thinking:

TAKE FROM RESULT UNKNOWN

4. Todd drank a pint of milk in the morning. He drank another pint in the afternoon and pint in the evening. How many ounces of milk did he drink? Did he drink at least a quart?

Way#1: Solve with a drawing

Way#2: Solve with an equation, use a letter for the unknown

Explain your thinking:

Problem Solving with Math Models© 2012

TAKE FROM RESULT UNKNOWN

5. Stephanie wanted to exercise for 2 hours. She spent 27 minutes on the treadmill, 45 minutes on the bicycle, and 15 minutes lifting weights. How many more minutes does she need to exercise to complete a 2 hour exercise routine?

Solve with an open number line diagram

Explain your thinking:

TAKE FROM RESULT UNKNOWN

6. The bakery sold 14 ounces of fudge in the morning, 5 ounces in the afternoon, and 8 ounces in the evening. How many ounces of fudge did they sell that day? Did they sell more than a pound?

Way#1: Model with a tape diagram

Way#2: Solve with an equation, use a letter for the unknown

Explain your thinking:

TAKE FROM RESULT UNKNOWN

7. Farmer Clark made a square cage for his chickens. The sides were 10 ft. long. The cage was too big, so he shortened the sides by 3 ft. each. How long was each new side? What is the new area and the new perimeter?

Way#1: Solve with a drawing

Way#2: Solve with the formulas for perimeter and area. Show all your work.

Explain your thinking:

TAKE FROM RESULT UNKNOWN

8. Grace wanted to run a mile. She ran ¼ of a mile in the morning and 2/4 of a mile in the afternoon. How far did she run? How much farther does she have to run to complete her 1-mile goal in the evening?

Way#1: Draw a picture to solve

Way#2: Solve with an equation, use a letter for the unknown

Explain your thinking:

Problem Solving with Math Models© 2012

CHAPTER 1 QUIZ:
TAKE FROM RESULT UNKNOWN PROBLEMS

Solve with a model:

1.   Joshua had $154. He spent $24 on games, $56 on shoes, and $59 on clothes. How much money did he have left?

2.   The fruit stand had 2 kilos of apples. They sold 500 grams in the morning and 1000 more grams in the afternoon. How many grams of apples did they have left?

3. Lucinda had 2 meters of string. She used 78 centimeters to make a necklace and 55 centimeters to make a bracelet. How many centimeters of string did she have left? Does she have at least a meter left?

4. Fay had 3 hours to stay at the mall. She spent 90 minutes at the movies, 25 minutes in the arcade and 15 minutes in the candy store. How much time does she have left?

Problem Solving with Math Models© 2012

CHAPTER 2
TAKE FROM CHANGE UNKNOWN PROBLEMS

In these problems students are looking for what happened in the middle of the story. In this type of story we know what happened at the beginning but then some change happened and now we have less than we started with by the end of the story. We are trying to find out how many things were taken away in the middle of the story.

PROBLEM	John had 15 marbles. He gave some to his cousin. Now he has 12 left. How many did he give to his cousin?
MODEL	
EQUATION	15 – ? = 12

TAKE FROM CHANGE UNKNOWN

1. Greg ran 2/3 of a mile in the morning. He ran some more in the afternoon. In total, he ran a mile. How far did he run in the afternoon?

Way#1: Solve with a number line

Way#2: Solve with an equation, use a letter for the unknown

Explain your thinking:

Take from Change Unknown

2. Lilia left her house at 3:15 p.m. She came back at 5:30 p.m. How long was she gone?

Solve with a number line diagram

Explain your thinking:

TAKE FROM CHANGE UNKNOWN

3. Tom the baker used 256 grams of sugar in his pie recipe. Then he used some more sugar for a cake. In total he used 302 grams of sugar. How many grams of sugar did he use for a cake?

Way#1: Model with a tape diagram

Way#2: Solve with an equation, use a letter for the unknown

Explain your thinking:

TAKE FROM CHANGE UNKNOWN

4. Grandma Betsy made a delicious fruit punch. She made 2 liters of punch. Her grandchildren drank 700 ml in the morning, 500 ml in the afternoon, and some more in the evening. At the end of the day, she had 235 ml left. How many more ml did her grandchildren drink in the evening?

Way#1: Model with a tape diagram

Way#2: Solve with an equation, use a letter for the unknown

Explain your thinking:

TAKE FROM CHANGE UNKNOWN

5. The store had 3 meters of string for sale. Customer 1 bought 125 cm, Customer 2 bought 107 cm, and Customer 3 bought some as well. Altogether, the store sold 280 cm of string. How much string did Customer Three buy? How many meters did the store sell?

Way#1: Solve with an open number line

Way#2: Solve with an equation, use a letter for the unknown

Explain your thinking:

TAKE FROM CHANGE UNKNOWN

6. The length of the fence was originally 12 ft. long. The width was 9 feet long. Dan shortened the fence. Now it is only 7 ft. long. By how much did Dan shorten the fence? What is the new perimeter? What is the new area?

Way#1: Solve with a drawing

Way#2: Solve with the formulas

Explain your thinking:

TAKE FROM CHANGE UNKNOWN

7. Kerry made a pizza. At first, he used 2/7 of a cup of yellow cheese. Then he added some more. Altogether, he used 5/7 cup of cheese on the pizza. How much cheese did he did he add to the pizza?

Way#1: Solve with an open number line

Way#2: Solve with an illustration

Explain your thinking:

Take From Change Unknown

8.   Nancy had $405. She spent $105 on shoes, $227 on clothes, and some more money on jewelry. She spent $380. How much did she spend on jewelry? How much does she have left?

Way#1: Model with a tape diagram

Way#2: Solve with an equation, use a letter for the unknown

Explain your thinking:

CHAPTER 2 QUIZ:
TAKE FROM CHANGE UNKNOWN PROBLEMS

Solve with a model:

1. Mark had 87 trading cards. He gave 15 to his brother, 18 to his cousin, and some to his friend. He gave a total of 42 trading cards away. How many trading cards did he give to his friend? How many does he have left?

2. Baker Daniel had 3 pounds of butter. He used 9 ounces for some cookies, 8 ounces for some cakes, and 7 ounces for some pies. How many ounces of butter did he have left?

3. Mr. Vega left his house at 2:17 p.m. He came back at 5:02 p.m. How long was he gone?

4. Tamara had $91. She spent $27 on jewelry, $28 on clothes, and some more money on shoes. She spent $82 in all. How much did she spend on shoes? How much did she have left?

CHAPTER 3
TAKE FROM START UNKNOWN PROBLEMS

In these problems students are looking for how many things there were at the beginning of the story. In this type of story we only know that there was some amount and that there was a change (some things were taken away). We know what was taken away and how much was left. We are trying to find out how much we had in the beginning of the story.

PROBLEM	John had some marbles. He gave his brother 5. Now he has 10 left. How many did he have in the beginning?
MODEL	
EQUATION	? - 5 = 10 15 - 5 = 10

Problem Solving with Math Models© 2012

TAKE FROM START UNKNOWN

1. Taylor spent $45 on shoes, $86 on clothes, and $48 on jewelry. She had $19 left. How much money did she have in the beginning?

Way#1: Solve with an open number line

Way#2: Solve with an equation, use a letter for the unknown

Explain your thinking:

TAKE FROM START UNKNOWN

2. Grandpa Ben drank some milk in the morning. He drank 450 ml of milk in the afternoon and 289 of milk in the evening. Altogether he drank 900 ml of milk. How much milk did he drink in the morning?

Way#1: Solve with a drawing

Way#2: Solve with an equation, use a letter for the unknown

Explain your thinking:

TAKE FROM START UNKNOWN

3. Grandma Betsy baked all morning. She used some flour for her cake, 350 grams of flour for her pies, and 276 grams of flour for her cookies. She used 1 kilogram of flour in total. How many grams of flour did she use for her cake?

Way#1: Solve with a tape diagram

Way#2: Solve with an equation, use a letter for the unknown

Explain your thinking:

TAKE FROM START UNKNOWN

4. Mary ate some pizza for lunch. She ate 2/4 of a pizza for dinner. She ate a total of ¾ of a pizza. How much pizza did she have for lunch?

Way#1: Solve with a number line

Way#2: Solve with an illustration

Explain your thinking:

TAKE FROM START UNKNOWN

5. Carlos had some marbles. He gave Jose 9 marbles. He gave his brother 12 marbles. Now he has 56 marbles left. How many marbles did he have to start with?

Way#1: Model with a tape diagram

Way#2: Solve with numbers

Explain your thinking:

Take from Start Unknown

6. Jessica had some string. She used 24 inches to make a necklace, 18 inches to make a bracelet, and 3 inches to make a ring. She had 15 inches of string left. How much string did she have in the beginning? Did she use more than a yard to make her jewelry?

Way#1: Solve with a tape diagram

Way#2: Solve with numbers

Explain your thinking:

Problem Solving with Math Models© 2012

TAKE FROM START UNKNOWN

7. Clint left his house early. He went to the store for 45 minutes. Then he went to his friend's house for 1 hour. Finally, he went to the park for 10 minutes. He got home at 3:15 p.m. What time did he leave his house?

Solve with a number line diagram

Explain your thinking:

TAKE FROM START UNKNOWN

8. Mike drank some orange juice in the morning. He drank 450 ml in the afternoon. He drank 489 more in the evening. Altogether, he drank 1078 ml of orange juice. How much orange juice did he drink in the morning? Did he drink more than a liter?

Way#1: Solve with a tape diagram

Way#2: Solve with numbers

Explain your thinking:

CHAPTER 3 QUIZ: TAKE FROM START UNKNOWN PROBLEMS

Solve with a model:

1. On Monday, some people listened to Song A. On Tuesday, 2,345,687 more people listened to Song A. By Wednesday morning, 3,456,909 people had listened to Song A. How many people had listened to Song A on Monday?

2. Ben ran in the morning. In the afternoon, he ran 2/5 of a mile more. By the evening, he ran 5/5 of a mile. How far had he run in the morning?

3. The candy store sold some chocolate in the morning. In the afternoon, they sold 500 more grams of it. In total, they sold 1 kilogram of chocolate. How much did they sell in the morning?

4. Mr. Griggs had some money. He spent $149 on shoes, $40 on a tie, $28 on a wallet, and $367 on clothes. He had $17 left. How much money did he have in the beginning?

UNIT 2 TEST:
TAKE FROM PROBLEMS

Solve with a model:

1. Manny had a small pizza. He at 1/8 of the pizza in the morning and 2/8 of the pizza in the afternoon. He ate 3/8 of the pizza in the evening. How much pizza did he eat altogether?

2. Hallie had some money. She spent $167 on jewelry, $78 on shoes, $109 on clothes, and $16 on candy. She has $35 left. How much did she have in the beginning?

3. Grandma Mabel had 500 grams of sugar. She used 349 grams in her cookies. Then she used some more for muffins. In total, she used 475 grams of sugar. How much sugar did she use for the muffins? How much did she have left?

4. Kelly arrived at the mall at 3:10 p.m. She left her house 25 minutes earlier. What time did she leave her house?

CHAPTER 1
PUT TOGETHER/TAKE APART PROBLEMS

These types of problems are about sets of things. In them we know both parts and we are looking for the whole. What distinguishes a Put Together/Take Apart Problem from an Add to Result Unknown problem is action. In a Put together/Take Apart Problem there is no action, only a set of something.

PROBLEM	John had five red apples and five green ones. How many apples did he have altogether?
MODEL	
EQUATION	5 + 5 = 10

Put Together/Take Apart—Whole Unknown

1. This weekend in our city, 46,345 people went to see Movie A. There were a total of 29,999 people that went to see Movie B. How many people went to see these two movies?

Way#1: Solve using any method

Way#2: Check your answer in a different way

Explain your thinking:

PUT TOGETHER/TAKE APART - WHOLE UNKNOWN

2. Sue built a fence. The length was 8 ft. The width was 5 ft. What was the perimeter? What was the area?

Way#1: Solve with a drawing

Way#2: Solve with the formulas

Explain your thinking:

PUT TOGETHER/TAKE APART—WHOLE UNKNOWN

3. John and his math partner were trying to solve an angle problem. They knew that one angle was 50 degrees, the other was 80 degrees and the other was 50. What was the total number of degrees of the angles in the triangle?

Solve with a number line diagram

Explain your thinking:

PUT TOGETHER/TAKE APART - WHOLE UNKNOWN

4. Sue biked 1/6 of a mile in the morning, 2/6 of a mile in the afternoon, and 3/6 of a mile in the evening. How far did Sue bike altogether? Did she bike at least a mile?

Way#1: Solve with a number line

Way#2: Solve with an equation, use a letter for the unknown

Explain your thinking:

PUT TOGETHER/TAKE APART—WHOLE UNKNOWN

5. Grandma Betsy used 378 grams of sugar in her first pie, 234 grams in her second, and 698 grams in her third. How many grams of sugar did she use in her pies? Did she use more or less than a kilogram of sugar?

Way#1: Solve with a tape diagram

Way#2: Solve with an equation, use a letter for the unknown

Explain your thinking:

PUT TOGETHER/TAKE APART—WHOLE UNKNOWN

6. Sue left her house at 2:10 p.m. She spent 45 minutes at her aunt's house and 45 minutes at her grandmother's house. How long was she out visiting? What time did she get back home?

Solve with an open number line diagram

Explain your thinking:

PUT TOGETHER/TAKE APART - WHOLE UNKNOWN

7. Grandpa Raul made a fruit punch for his grandkids. He used 1 liter of pineapple juice, 500 ml of apple juice, 359 ml of grape juice, and 876 ml of orange juice. How many milliliters of fruit punch did he make? How many liters of fruit punch did he make?

Way#1: Solve with a tape diagram

Way#2: Solve with numbers

Explain your thinking:

PUT TOGETHER/TAKE APART—WHOLE UNKNOWN

8. Macy wanted to exercise for 1 hour. She spent 23 minutes on the bike, 19 minutes on the treadmill, and 20 minutes weight lifting. How many minutes did she exercise? Did she complete an hour of exercise?

Way#1: Solve with an open number line

Way#2: Solve with an equation, use a letter for the unknown

Explain your thinking:

Chapter 1 Quiz: Put Together/ Take Apart – Whole Unknown Problems

Solve with a model:

1. Tom's grandpa gave him 4/10 of a dollar. His grandma gave him 50/100 of a dollar. How much money did they give him in total?

2. The candy store made some fudge. They made 234 grams of chocolate fudge, 457 grams of vanilla fudge, and 420 grams of peanut butter fudge. How many grams of fudge did they make altogether? Did they make more or less than a kilogram of fudge?

3. Kayla got some money for her birthday. Her grandma gave her $21.80. Her dad gave her $15.00. Her sister gave her $17.10. How much did she get for her birthday?

4. Chef Hugo used 1 kilogram of chocolate to bake. He then used another 500 grams of chocolate to make a sauce for his chicken. How many grams of chocolate did he use altogether?

CHAPTER 2
PUT TOGETHER/TAKE APART PROBLEMS PART UNKNOWN

These types of problems are about sets of things. In them we know the total and one part of the set. We are looking for the other part of the set.

PROBLEM	John had ten apples. Five were red apples and the rest were green. How many apples were green?
MODEL	
EQUATION	5 + 5 = 10

Put Together/Take Apart - Part Unknown

1. The fruit stand had 100 apples. Half of them were red and the other half green. How many were green?

Way#1: Solve with a number line

Way#2: Solve with an equation, use a letter for the unknown

Explain your thinking:

Put Together/Take Apart - Part Unknown

2. Tina spent $498. She spent $273 on clothes, $99 on shoes, $28 on jewelry and the rest on perfume. How much did she spend on perfume?

Way#1: Model with a tape diagram

Way#2: Solve with numbers

Explain your thinking:

Problem Solving with Math Models© 2012

PUT TOGETHER/TAKE APART - PART UNKNOWN

3. Twenty thousand people went to the movies this weekend. 7,349 people went to see comedies. 8,459 people went to see horror movies and the rest went to see action movies. How many people went to see action movies?

Way#1: Solve with numbers

Way#2: Check your answer a different way

Explain your thinking:

PUT TOGETHER/TAKE APART - PART UNKNOWN

4. The farm had 12 rabbits. One-fourth of them were black, one-fourth of them were white, and the rest were brown. What fraction of the rabbits were brown? How many were brown?

Way#1: Solve with a drawing

Way#2: Solve with an equation, use a letter for the unknown

Explain your thinking:

Put Together/Take Apart - Part Unknown

5. Jamal and his partner were working on a math problem. They were looking at a triangle. They knew that one angle measured 25 degrees and the other measured 75 degrees. How much did the 3rd angle measure?

Solve with a number line

Explain your thinking:

PUT TOGETHER/TAKE APART—PART UNKNOWN

6. Grandma Betsy used 1 kilogram of sugar for her cookies. She used 456 grams in her sugar cookies and the rest in her chocolate chip cookies. How many grams of sugar did she use in her chocolate chip cookies?

Way#1: Model with a tape diagram

Way#2: Solve with numbers

Explain your thinking:

Problem Solving with Math Models© 2012

PUT TOGETHER/TAKE APART - PART UNKNOWN

7. Anna made 2 liters of fruit punch. She used 800 ml of orange juice, 203 ml of pineapple juice, 259 ml of apple juice, and 175 ml of cherry juice. The rest of the fruit punch was banana juice. How many ml was banana juice?

Way#1: Model with a tape diagram

Way#2: Solve with an equation, use a letter for the unknown

Explain your thinking:

Put Together/Take Apart - Part Unknown

8. Jimmy built a rectangular fence with a perimeter of 30 ft. The length was 10 feet. What was the width? What was the area?

Way#1: Model with a drawing

Way#2: Solve using the formula for area

Explain your thinking:

CHAPTER 2 QUIZ:
PUT TOGETHER/TAKE APART - PART UNKNOWN

Solve with a model.

1. Dana had $456. She spent $88 on earrings, $43 on necklaces, $235 on clothes, and the rest on shoes. How much did she spend on shoes?

2. Chef Sue made a pie. She used 500 grams of sugar. She used 345 grams of white sugar and the rest was brown sugar. How much brown sugar did she use?

3. John drank 1 liter of apple juice. He drank 146 ml in the morning, 256 ml in the afternoon, and the rest in the evening. How many ml did he drink in the evening?

4. Jackson cut 3 meters of wood. First, he cut 59 centimeters, then he cut another 128 centimeters, and then he cut the rest. How many more centimeters of wood did he cut?

UNIT 3 TEST
PUT TOGETHER/TAKE APART TEST

Solve with a model.

1. Farmer Jamie is building a pen for his chickens. The original pen was 8 feet long and 9 feet wide. He realized that it was too small. So he added 3 feet to the length. What is the length of the new pen? What is the perimeter of the new pen? What is the area of the new pen?

2. Chris ran 2 miles. He ran 5/8 of a mile in the morning, 7/8 of a mile in the afternoon and the rest in the evening. How far did he run in the evening?

3. Mom and Julie are making some baked items for the school bake sale. They use 360 grams of sugar in their cupcakes and twice as much in a large cake. How much sugar did they use in the cake? How much sugar did they use altogether?

4. The trip from Sam's house to the library is one mile. On the way, he passes a school and a firehouse. From his house to the school it's 2/8 of a mile. From the school to the firehouse it's another 5/8 of a mile. Next stop is the library. How far is it from the firehouse to the library?

Problem Solving with Math Models© 2012

CHAPTER 1
COMPARE DIFFERENCE UNKNOWN

In these problems students are comparing two or more amounts. They are comparing to find out what is the difference between the amounts. There are two versions of this type of story. One version uses the word more and one version uses the word fewer. The version with the word fewer is more difficult.

PROBLEM MORE VERSION	John had 12 marbles. Carl had 2 marbles. How many more marbles does John have than Carl?
MODEL	John Difference is 10 Carl 2 12
EQUATION	2 + ? = 12 2 + 10 =12

PROBLEM FEWER VERSION	Carl had 2 marbles. John had 12 marbles. How many fewer marbles does Carl have than John?
MODEL	John Carl
EQUATION	12 – 2 =? 12 – 2 = 10

COMPARE FRACTIONS

1. Tim ate 2/3 of a small pizza. Clark ate 1/3 of a small pizza. How much more pizza did Tim eat than Clark?

Way#1: Solve with pictures

Way#2: Solve with a number line

Explain your thinking:

COMPARE FRACTIONS

2. Tommy ate 5/6 of his candy bar. Kayla at 6/6 of hers. If the candy bars were the same size, who ate more?

Way#1: Solve with a number line

Way#2: Show the relationship with the symbols
       <, >, or =

Explain your thinking:

COMPARE FRACTIONS

3. Jose jogged 2/4 of a mile this morning. Tom jogged 1/2 of a mile this afternoon. Who ran farther?

Way#1: Solve with an illustration

Way#2: Solve with a number line

Explain your thinking:

COMPARE USING LINE PLOTS

4. Here are the lengths (in feet) of several pieces of string that were cut.

    1/8, 1/8, 2/8, 3/8, 3/8, 3/8, 4/8, 1/2, 1/2,1/2, 1/2,1/2

Make a line plot for the data

Question 1: What was the total amount of the 1/8 ft. ribbons cut?

Question 2: What was the difference between the shortest and longest ribbons?

COMPARE USING LINE PLOT

5. These are the lengths (in inches) of various flowers that grew in the garden last week.

    1/4, 1/4, 1/4, 2/4, 2/4, 2/4, 3/4, 3/4, 3/4, 3/4, 3/4

Make a line plot for the data

Question 1: **What is the total length of the flowers that grew 2/4 of an inch?**

Question 2: **What is the difference between the shortest length and the tallest length that the flowers grew?**

COMPARE DIFFERENCE UNKNOWN

6. Susie had $0.60 and Don had $0.55. Who had more money? How much more?

Way#1: Illustrate with money

Way#2: Compare the decimals with symbols
        <,>, or =

Explain your thinking:

COMPARE DIFFERENCE UNKNOWN

7. In one hour, on the internet 7,500 people like Video A, but only 2,578 people liked Video B. How many more people liked Video A than liked Video B? How many people liked for the videos altogether?

Way#1: Solve with numbers

Way#2: Record the results of comparisons with symbols <, >, or = and justify with a model

Explain your thinking:

Problem Solving with Math Models© 2012

COMPARE DIFFERENCE UNKNOWN

8. Mara drew an acute angle. Carol drew a right angle. Whose angle was larger?

Way#1: Solve with an illustration

Way#2: Compare with symbols

Explain your thinking:

CHAPTER 1 QUIZ: COMPARE PROBLEMS

Solve with a model:

1. In 1 hour, 4,908 people voted for Song A on the internet. Only 3,999 people voted for Song B. How many fewer people voted for Song B than liked Song A? How many people voted altogether?

2. John had 50/100 of a dollar. Tom had 6/10 of a dollar. Who had more? How much more?

Problem Solving with Math Models© 2012

3. Chef Juan used 567 grams of sugar for his sweet potato pie and 489 grams of sugar for his pineapple cake. How much less sugar did he use for his pineapple cake than for his sweet potato pie?

4. Kayla ate 1/5 of her candy bar. Luke at 5/5 of his candy bar. If the candy bars were the same size, who ate more? How much more?

CHAPTER 2
COMPARISON – BIGGER PART UNKNOWN

In these problems students are comparing two or more amounts. They are comparing to find out who had the bigger part. There are two versions of this type of story. One version uses the word more and one version uses the word fewer. The version with the word *fewer* is considered to be more difficult.

PROBLEM MORE VERSION	John has 5 more marbles than Carl. Carl has 2 marbles. How many marbles does John have?
MODEL	John 7 total Carl
EQUATION	2 + 5 = ? 2 + 5 = 7

PROBLEM FEWER VERSION	Carl has 3 fewer marbles than John? Carl has 2 marbles. How many marbles does John have?
MODEL	Carl John 5 total
	2 + 3 = ? 2 + 3 = 5

COMPARISON – BIGGER PART UNKNOWN

1. The candy store sold 459 grams of chocolate fudge. It sold 379 more grams of strawberry swirl fudge. How much strawberry swirl fudge did it sell?

Way#1: Solve with a double number line

Way#2: Record the results of comparisons with symbols <, >, or = and justify with a model

Explain your thinking:

COMPARISON – BIGGER PART UNKNOWN

2. Grandpa Ben used 289 grams of sugar in his apple pie and 240 more grams of sugar in his pineapple cake. How many grams of sugar did he use in his pineapple cake?

Way#1: Model with a tape diagram

Way#2: Record the results of comparisons with symbols <, >, or = and justify with a model

Explain your thinking:

Problem Solving with Math Models© 2012

COMPARISON – BIGGER PART UNKNOWN

3. Emily drank 2 pints of orange juice. Carol drank 2 more pints of orange juice than Emily did. How many more cups of orange juice did Carol drink than Emily? Did Carol drink a quart of orange juice?

Way#1: Solve with pictures

Way#2: Record the results of comparisons with symbols <, >, or = and justify with a model

Explain your thinking:

COMPARISON – BIGGER PART UNKNOWN

4. Jonathan drank 398 ml of milk in the morning. Jamal drank 349 more ml of milk than Jonathan. Did he drink more or less than a liter or milk?

Way#1: Solve with an illustration

Way#2: Record the results of comparisons with symbols <, >, or = and justify with a model

Explain your thinking:

COMPARISON – BIGGER PART UNKNOWN

5. Miguel had \$23.45. Luke had \$10.40 more than Miguel did. How much money did Luke have?

Way#1: Solve with numbers

Way#2: Record the results of comparisons with symbols <, >, or = and justify with a model

Explain your thinking:

COMPARISON – BIGGER PART UNKNOWN

6. Yanni ran ¼ of a mile. Luke ran 2/4 of a mile farther than Yanni. How far did Luke run?

Way#1: Solve with a double number line

Way#2: Record the results of comparisons with symbols <, >, or = and justify with a model

Explain your thinking:

COMPARISON – BIGGER PART UNKNOWN

7. The toy store has 89 red marbles, 34 multicolored marbles, and 56 black marbles. There are ten more green marbles than black marbles. There are twenty more purple marbles than the red and multicolored marbles combined. How many green marbles are there? How many purple marbles are there? How many marbles are there altogether?

Way#1: Model with a tape diagram

Way#2: Solve with numbers

Explain your thinking:

COMPARISON – BIGGER PART UNKNOWN

8. Carl drank 856 ml of orange juice. He drank 78 fewer ml fewer than Ricky. How many ml of orange juice did Ricky drink?

Way#1: Solve with a double number line

Way#2: Record the results of comparisons with symbols <, >, or = and justify with a model

Explain your thinking:

Problem Solving with Math Models© 2012

CHAPTER 2 QUIZ:
COMPARE BIGGER PART UNKNOWN

Solve with a model:

1. Mark at 2/12 of his candy bar. Miguel at 6/12 more of his candy bar than Mark did of his. The candy bars were the same size. How much of his candy bar did Miguel eat?

2. Song A has 28,345 votes. It has 3,500 fewer votes than Song B. How many votes does Song B have?

3. The bakery used 589 grams of sugar for cookies. It used 378 more grams of sugar for doughnuts than for cookies. How many grams of sugar did it use for doughnuts? How many grams of sugar did it use altogether?

4. Harry drank 508 ml of milk. His brother drank 100 more ml than he did. His cousin drank 358 more ml than his brother did. How much did his brother drink? How much did his cousin drink? Did anyone drink more than a liter? If so, who?

CHAPTER 3
COMPARISON – SMALLER PART UNKNOWN

In these problems students are comparing two or more amounts. They are comparing to find out who has the smaller amount. There are two versions of this type of story. One version uses the word more and one version uses the word fewer. The version with the word *more* is considered to be more difficult.

PROBLEM MORE VERSION	John had 4 more marbles than Carl. John had 5 marbles. How many marbles did Carl have?
MODEL	John ⬤ ⬤ ⬤ ⬤⬤ Carl ⬤
EQUATION	5 – 4 = ? 5 – 4 =1

PROBLEM FEWER VERSION	Carl had 10 fewer marbles than John. John had 12 marbles. How many marbles did Carl have?
MODEL	
EQUATION	12 – 10 = x 12 – 10 = 2

COMPARISON – SMALLER PART UNKNOWN

1. Luke ate 2/4 of a candy bar. John ate ¼ less than Luke did. The candy bars were the same size. How much of the candy bar did John eat?

Way#1: Solve with a double number line

Way#2: Solve with an equation, use a letter for the unknown

Explain your thinking:

COMPARISON – SMALLER PART UNKNOWN

2. Becky made some cookies. She put 456 grams of flour in the chocolate chip cookies. She put 100 more grams of flour in the chocolate chip cookies than in the peanut butter cookies. How much flour did she put in the peanut butter cookies?

Way#1: Model with a tape diagram

Way#2: Solve with an equation, use a letter for the unknown

Explain your thinking:

COMPARISON – SMALLER PART UNKNOWN

3. Song A has 15,299 downloads. Song B has 1,645 fewer downloads than Song A. How many downloads does Song B have?

Way#1: Solve with numbers

Way#2: Check a different way

Explain your thinking:

COMPARISON – SMALLER PART UNKNOWN

4. Lucy made a great fruit punch. She used 345 ml of pineapple juice and 204 fewer ml of apple juice. How much apple juice did she use?

Way#1: Solve with drawing

Way#2: Solve with an equation, use a letter for the unknown

Explain your thinking:

COMPARISON – SMALLER PART UNKNOWN

5. Mr. Robinson planted 2 gardens. Garden A had a length of 6 ft. and a width of 7 ft. The length of Garden B was 1 ft. smaller than the length of Garden A and the width of Garden B was 2 ft. smaller than the width of Garden A. What was the perimeter of Garden A? What was the perimeter of Garden B?

Way#1: Model with a drawing

Way#2: Solve using the formulas for area and perimeter

Explain your thinking:

COMPARISON – SMALLER PART UNKNOWN

6. Henry had $45.76. His brother had $22.50 less than Henry. How much money did Henry's brother have?

Way#1: Solve with numbers

Way#2: Check in a different way

Explain your thinking:

COMPARISON – SMALLER PART UNKNOWN

7. Chef Luke used 1 lb. of butter in his special bread. He used 5 fewer ounces of butter in his pasta. How many ounces of butter did he use in his pasta?

Way #1: Model with a tape diagram

Way #2: Solve with numbers

Explain your thinking:

COMPARISON – SMALLER PART UNKNOWN

8. Luke cut 3 meters of wood. Hank cut 100 fewer cm than Luke did. How much wood did Hank cut?

Way#1: Model with a tape diagram

Way#2: Solve with numbers

Explain your thinking:

CHAPTER 3 QUIZ:
COMPARE SMALLER UNKNOWN PROBLEMS

Solve with a model:

1. The jewelry store had 145 silver rings. They had 34 fewer gold rings than silver ones. They had 10 fewer wooden rings than gold ones. How many gold rings did they have? How many wooden rings did they have?

2. Mrs. Thomas planted 2 gardens. Garden A was had a square perimeter of 24 ft. Garden B had a length 2 feet shorter than Garden A and a width 3 ft. shorter than Garden A. What was the perimeter of Garden B?

Problem Solving with Math Models© 2012

3.   Raul ran 3/4 of a mile. Frank ran 1/4 of a mile less than Raul. How far did Frank run?

4.   Sue had 4 meters of string. Ann had 200 fewer centimeters of string than Sue. How much string did Ann have?

Unit 4 Test:
Compare Problems

Solve with a model:

1. Kate ate 2/4 of her candy bar. Joe ate 3/4 of his. If the candy bars were the same size, who ate more? How much more?

2. Grandma Lily used 345 grams of flour in her lemon cake. She used 200 more grams of sugar in her peach cake than in her lemon cake. How many grams did she use in her peach cake? How many grams of sugar did she use for both cakes?

Problem Solving with Math Models© 2012

3. Joe ran 2/4 of a mile. John ran 1/4 of a mile more than Joe. Luke ran ¼ of a mile less than Joe. How far did John run? How far did Luke run? How far did they run altogether?

4. Mary went shopping. She spent $123 on perfume. She spent $100 more on a scarf than she did on perfume. She spent $20 less on earrings than she did on the scarf. How much did the scarf cost? How much did the earrings cost?

NAME:

DATE:

Solve the problems. Show your work by drawing a picture, using a number line, making a table, or using formulas.

1. Larry left his house at 5:15 p.m. He spent an hour and 15 minutes at Brian's house and an hour and a half at the basketball court. What time did he go home?

2. Don, the baker, used 25 grams of sugar in his cake mixture. Then he added 37 more grams of sugar. How many grams of sugar did he use for his cake?

3. Farmer Jane built a yard for her rabbits. First, she made a yard that was 8ft long and 9 ft. wide. Then she added some length to the fence. Now the length is 12 ft. long. How many feet did she add to the length? What is the new perimeter of the yard?

4. The school cook made some liters of fruit punch. He then made 4 more liters. Altogether, he made 20 liters of fruit punch. How much fruit punch did he make in the beginning?

5. Sara had 205 cm of string to make bracelets. She used 88 cm on Monday, 26 cm on Tuesday, 28 cm on Wednesday, and 14 cm on Thursday. How much string did she have left on Friday?

6. John left his house at 2:15 p.m. He came back at 5:55 p.m. How long was he gone?

Problem Solving with Math Models© 2012

7. The candy store sold 900 grams of chocolate in the morning, 180 grams in the afternoon, and some more in the evening. Altogether, they sold 2 kilograms of chocolate. How much did they sell in the evening?

8. Carl cooked all morning. He used some butter in the soup. In his bread, he used 12 more ounces of butter. In total, he used 1 pound of butter. How much butter did he put in the soup?

9. Ten thousand people went to the movies this weekend in our city. All total, 5,759 people went to see comedies, 3,489 people went to see dramas, and the rest went to see action movies. How many people went to see action movies?

10. Justin built a fence with a perimeter of 48 ft. The length was 12 feet. What was the width?

11. Tommy ate 1/6 of his candy bar. Kayla ate 5/6 of hers. If the candy bars were the same size, who ate more? How much more?

12. Paco used 140 ml of apple juice in his punch and 200 more ml of orange juice than apple juice. How much orange juice did he use?

13. Lucia's class cut several strips of ribbon. Here is the data (in inches) of the sizes.

3/4, 3/4, 3/4, 3/4, 3/4, 1/4, 1/4, 1/4, 1/4, 2/4, 2/4, 2/4, 2/4

Make a line plot

Question 1: How many people cut 3/4?

Question 2: How many people cut 1/4 inch of ribbon?

Question 3: How many people cut 1/2 an inch?

Problem Solving with Math Models© 2012

14. On the internet Song A got 15,991 votes in 1 hour. Song B got 2,347 fewer votes than Song A. How many votes did Song B get? How many people voted altogether?

15. John drew an acute angle and Clark drew an obtuse angle. Whose angle is larger?

Unit 1
Add to Problems

Chapter 1: Add to Result Unknown Problems
1. 52,844 downloads
2. 1 hour, 10 minutes
3. 1,085 grams; yes
4. 934 ml; no
5. $154.30
6. No, he ran exactly a mile
7. 46 ft.; 112 ft.
8.

Necklaces	Inches	Feet
1	12	1
2	24	2
3	36	3

Chapter 1 Quiz: Add to Result Unknown
1. 3 quarts; no
2. 30 ft.; 56 square ft.
3. 1,043 meters; yes
4. 9/6 or 1 ½ yards; yes

Chapter 2: Add to Change Unknown Problems
1. 565 grams; yes
2. 1 hour, 52 minutes
3. 3/6 or ½ of a mile
4. 600 ml of apple juice
5. $17.05
6. 45 centimeters
7. 6 ft.; 34 ft.
8. 13 ounces

Chapter 2 Quiz: Add to Change Unknown Problem
1. 2 hours, 28 minutes
2. 22 kilos
3. 2/5 of a mile
4. $27.02

Chapter 3: Add to Start Unknown
1. 10,531 downloads
2. 11:30
3. ¼ mile
4. $12.11
5. 55 liters
6. 12 marbles
7. 1 ½ cups of apples
8. 2/7 of a mile

Chapter 3 Quiz: Add to Start Unknown Problems
1. 118 centimeters; 1 meter, 18 cm
2. 1:55
3. 467 ml; yes
4. 3 kilometers

UNIT 1 TEST: ADDITION PROBLEMS
1. 220 rings
2. 6/6 or 1 mile; yes
3. 22 ft.; 28 square feet
4. 151 grams;

Unit 2
Take From Problems

Chapter 1: Take From Result Unknown
1. $52
2. 246 grams; yes
3.

Shelves	Centimeters	Meters
1	100	1
2	200	2
3	300	3
4	400	4
5	500	5

4. 48 ounces; yes
5. 33 more minutes
6. 27 ounces; yes
7. 7 ft.; 49 square ft.; 28 ft.
8. ¾ of a mile; ¼ of mile farther

Chapter 1 Quiz: Take From Result Unknown Problems
1. $15
2. 500 grams
3. 67 centimeters; no
4. 50 min.

Chapter 2: Take From Change Unknown Problems
1. 1/3 of a mile
2. 2 hours, 15 minutes
3. 46 grams of sugar
4. 565 ml
5. 58 cm; 2 meters, 80 cm
6. 10 ft.; 32 ft.; 63 square ft.
7. 3/7 of a cup
8. $48; $25

Chapter 2 Quiz: Take From Change Unknown Problems
1. 9 trading cards; 45 left
2. 24 ounces
3. 2 hours, 45 minutes
4. $27; $9

Chapter 3: Take From Start Unknown Problems
1. $198
2. 161 ml
3. 374 grams
4. ¼ of the pizza
5. 77 marbles
6. 60 inches; yes
7. 1:20
8. 139 ml; yes

Chapter 3 Quiz: Take From Start Unknown Problems
1. 1,111,222 people
2. 3/5 of a mile
3. 500 grams
4. $601

UNIT 2 TEST: TAKE FROM PROBLEMS
1. 6/8 or ¾ of the pizza
2. $405
3. 126 grams; 25 grams
4. 2:45

Answer Key

Unit 3
Put Together/Take Apart Problems

Chapter 1: Put Together/Take Apart— Whole Unknown Problems
1. 76,344 people
2. 26 ft.; 40 square feet
3. 180 degrees
4. 6/6 of a mile or 1 mile; yes
5. 1,310 grams; more than a kilogram
6. 1 hour, 30 minutes; 3:40
7. 2,735 ml; 2 liters, 735 ml
8. 62 minutes; yes

Chapter 1 Quiz: Put Together/Take Apart—Whole Unknown Problems
1. 90 cents
2. 1,111 grams; more than a kilogram
3. $53.90
4. 1500 grams

Chapter 2: Put Together/Take Apart— Part Unknown Problems
1. 50 green apples
2. $98
3. 4,192 people
4. 6 rabbits
5. 80 degrees
6. 544 grams
7. 563 ml
8. 5 ft.; 50 square feet

Chapter 2 Quiz: Put Together/Take Apart—Part Unknown Problems
1. $90
2. 155 grams
3. 598 ml
4. 113 centimeters

UNIT 3 TEST: PUT TOGETHER/TAKE APART PROBLEMS
1. 11 ft.; 40 ft.; 99 square ft.
2. 4/8 of a mile
3. 720 grams; 1,080 grams
4. 1/8 of a mile

Unit 4
Comparison - Difference Unknown Problems

Chapter 1: Compare Fraction Problems
1. 1/3 more of the pizza
2. Kayla
3. They ran the same distance
4. 2/8 or ¼ feet; 3/8 of a foot
5. 6/4 or 1 2/4 or 1 ½ inches; 2/4 or ½ an inch
6. Susie; $0.05 more
7. 4,922 more people; 10,078 people voted
8. Carl's angle

Chapter 1 Quiz: Compare Problems
1. 909 fewer people; 8,907 people voted
2. Tom; 10 cents more
3. 78 fewer grams
4. Luke; 4/5 more

Problem Solving with Math Models© 2012

Chapter 2: Comparison—Bigger Part Unknown Problems

1. 838 grams
2. 529 grams
3. 4 more cups; yes
4. 747 ml; less
5. $33.85
6. ¾ of a mile
7. 66 green marbles; 143 purple marbles; 388 marbles in all
8. 934 ml

Chapter 2 Quiz: Comparison—Bigger Part Unknown Problems

1. 8/12 or 2/3 of the candy bar
2. 31,845 votes
3. 967 grams; 1556 g
4. 608 ml; 966 ml; no

Chapter 3: Comparison—Smaller Part Unknown Problems

1. ¼ of the candy bar
2. 356 grams
3. 13,654 downloads
4. 141 ml
5. 26 ft.; 20 ft.
6. $23.26
7. 11 ounces
8. 200 centimeters or 2 meters

Chapter 3 Quiz: Comparison Smaller Unknown Problems

1. 111 gold rings; 101 wooden rings
2. 14 ft.
3. 2/4 or ½ of a mile
4. 200 centimeters or 2 meters

UNIT 4 TEST: COMPARE PROBLEMS

1. Joe; ¼ more
2. 545 grams; 890 grams
3. ¾; ¼; 6/4 or 1 ½ miles
4. $223; $203

Final Word Problem Test

1. 8:00
2. 62 grams
3. 4 ft.; 42 ft.
4. 16 liters
5. 49 cm
6. 3 hours, 40 minutes
7. 920 grams
8. 4 ounces
9. 752 people
10. 12 feet
11. Kayla; 4/6 more
12. 340 ml
13. 5; 4; 4
14. 13.644 votes; 29,635 people voted
15. Clark's angle is larger

REFERENCES

Charles, R. *Solving Word Problems: Developing Students' Quantitative Reasoning Abilities* http://assets.pearsonschool.com/asset_mgr/legacy/200931/Problem%20Solving%20Monograph_24324_1.pdf

Carpenter, T., Fennema, E., Franke, M., Levi, L., & Empson, S. (1999). *Children's Mathematics: Cognitively Guided Instruction.* Portsmouth, NH: Heinemann.

Common Core Standards Writing Team (Bill McCullum, lead author). (2012, June 23). *Progressions for the common core state standards in mathematics: Geometry (draft).* Retrieved from: www.commoncoretools.wordpress.com.

Common Core Standards Writing Team (Bill McCullum, lead author). (2012, June 23). *Progressions for the common core state standards in mathematics: Geometric measurement (draft).* Retrieved from: www.commoncoretools.wordpress.com.

Common Core Standards Writing Team (Bill McCullum, lead author). (2011, June 20). *Progressions for the common core state standards in mathematics: K-3, Categorical data; Grades 2-5, Measurement Data (draft).* Retrieved from: www.commoncoretools.wordpress.com.

Common Core Standards Writing Team (Bill McCullum, lead author). (2011, May 29). *Progressions for the common core state standards in mathematics: K, Counting and cardinality; K-5, operations and algebraic thinking (draft).* Retrieved from: www.commoncoretools.wordpress.com.

Common Core Standards Writing Team (Bill McCullum, lead author). (2011, April 7). *Progressions for the common core state standards in mathematics: K-5, Number and operations in base ten (draft).* Retrieved from: www.commoncoretools.wordpress.com.

Common Core Standards Writing Team (Bill McCullum, lead author). (2011, July 12). *Progressions for the common core state standards in mathematics: 3-5 Number and operations - fractions (draft)*. Retrieved from: www.commoncoretools.wordpress.com.

Peterson, P. L., Carpenter, T. P., & Loef, M. (1989). *Teachers' Pedagogical Content Beliefs in Mathematics. Cognition and Instruction*, Vol. 6, No. 1, pp. 1-40.

Contact Us!

Dr. Nicki Newton

Email: gigglenook@gmail.com

Website: www.drnicki123.com

Blog: guidedmath.wordpress.com